Social Skil

MW00893313

The Ultimate Guide for Improve
Your Conversation and
Communication Skills, How to
Overcome Shyness with This Easy
Step-By-Step Course

Table of Contents

Introduction

Effective social and communication skills are non-negotiable in today's world. Unless you know how to navigate your way through various social situations with highly developed communication skills, you may end up underutilizing your potential or not being able to enjoy fulfilling interpersonal/social relationships or not being able to live your life to the fullest. People who master communication and social skills open up a world of opportunities for themselves. There is no limit to what you can accomplish if you develop confidence, social skills, and effective communication/interaction patterns.

The best thing is, even if you are not a communication pro or think you don't have the required confidence or charisma, it can be built (yes pretty much like your muscles). You can transform from a nervous communicator to confident, self-assured and assertive social being with consistent practice, effort and the invaluable strategies mentioned in this book. We are all inborn social beings and communicators. However, only a handful manages to harness their communication skills and turn it into their strength.

Ace social skills are the foundation of some of the strongest relationships, both personal and professional. Everyone digs and follows an awesome communicator. Look at any of the social media influencers and people with a large following. They will almost always know how to build rapport with their followers and build trust, which is why people will lap up everything they say. That's why Instagrammers are raking in cool millions through their endorsements and promotions. They are paid big bucks because they possess the ability to sway people towards a particular brand or decision based on their slick communication skills.

There is no escaping the fact that communication is needed in every sphere of our life from job interviews to impressing a date to networking to building an enviable social circle. Communication is one of the most vital productivity tools, helping you leave behind a favorable impression wherever you go. Just imagine having a brain brimming with ideas but unable to express those ideas. Wouldn't that be terrible? Communication is the muscle that awards us the power to convey our ideas in a compelling style, such that people are forced to sit up and take note.

Every relationship that we have in this world is somewhat determined by how the other person or we relate to us. It is impossible to fulfill all our requirements by ourselves. Relating to others or seeking help from them needs communication. Want to experience the effects of a lack of communication? Buy a ticket to a country whose local language you absolutely cannot comprehend. You'll realize how tough it is to express every tiny detail. It will be a mammoth task! Unless you and the other person are sign language experts, you'll have a tough time communicating even basic needs such as food or accommodation.

Effective communication skills equip a person with the ability to collaborate, exchange ideas, share views, and generally relate to their world. It makes the exchange of ideas less tough. The original superpower of humans is the gift of expressing their ideas, socializing and collaborating with each other. This is precisely what led to our progress with creations such as automobiles, roads and electrical gadgets. These things wouldn't have been possible without exchanging ideas and communicating concepts. Thus communication is permeable in every sphere of our life.

Now be honest, alright? Tell me when you are introduced to someone for the first time; on what basis do you form an impression about them without knowing anything about them. Naturally, through the way they are dressed or their communication skills, right? You hear them speak and go boom wow or ohhh no, right? You can also use effective communication skills to blow people away or influence/inspire them to do what you want. Yes, some people will use it for wrongdoing (think manipulation and deceiving people). However, it is largely a kick-ass skill that will help you become a mover and shaker of your professional and social circle faster than you can imagine. Once you master communication skills explained in this book, you'll wow people. Effective communicators are engaging, interesting and persuasive.

Make no mistake, though. Communication is not only about talking but also about being a great listener, practicing empathy and building rapport with others through trust. Think about what happens to our brain's ability to share ideas or complete tasks if we are unable to communicate. Why do you think some of the world's best salespersons will manage to sell a comb to a bald person? The answer is obvious – they possess the power to communicate effectively enough to convince their buyers that they even though they may not need the product, they will want to buy it. They make their products and services desirable and irresistible, in a manner in which it becomes almost impossible for the other person to refuse. It's happened countless times with us. We've bought things we don't even need simply because the salesperson sounded so damn convincing that refusing the product or service was not even an option.

Visualize a life where you are an incredible people magnet who holds a powerful influence and charm over others. Think how wonderful it would it is to have people holding on to every word you speak. Think how amazing it would be to leave people dazzled with your conversation skills. How about drawing people to you through empathy and exceptional listening skills? Think about the wonders of being a person whose company everyone craves and looks forward to. You will end up having an unspoken hold influence over others along with the power to build meaningful, fulfilling and highly beneficial relationships that help you meet your personal and professional goals. Communication is the master keys that are capable of unlocking your truest potential and connect with others. The world needs to see what you hold within, which is possible only through the power of communication.

What if you were told that you could indeed be all of this and much more? Of course, you can! Wherever you are hanging currently in your communication skills quotient, you have the power to be the Master of Social skill. Yes, even if you consider yourself the most awkward and terrible communicator in the world. With the right intention and effort, you won't just survive relationships; you will go about conquering them.

The power to communicate effectively with people in several scenarios reveals high social intelligence and communication proficiency. Behaving effectively in multiple social situations is the secret to a person's personal, professional and social success. You can have all the skills, qualification, gifts, technical finesse and experience.

However, if you are not an effective communicator, you reduce your success chances, unless you live in a rabbit hole where communication with people is not required. When we are unable to communicate with others, our bond of collaborations and associations weakens, thus inhibiting our success chances or the ability to live a fulfilling and meaningful life. Effective communication, therefore, is one of the biggest secrets to gaining success in every sphere of life.

Don't you as a customer get floored by a customer service representative who is able to not just understand your concern by keenly listening to you but also demonstrates empathy and resolves it for you? We all love to be understood. We love it when people actually listen to us as opposed to simply hearing what we speak.

According to a research study, enterprises with healthy and meaningful communication practices outperform their competitors by a good three and a half times. These are the companies that build solid teams, avoid misunderstandings, develop efficient customer service, negotiate beneficial deals and obtain feedback from their customers – all of which are factors that contribute to a smoothly functioning business. None of us here is operating from an isolated island without any human contact. We are surrounded by people and are constantly engaged in fulfilling their needs and getting them to fulfill our needs. A powerful, magnetic and engaging leader can inspire their team to run after their goals. You can get people to take the desired action if you are an effective and compelling leader.

Think about your favorite personality or entrepreneur. There are high chances that the person you've chosen as your idol is a top-class communicator. Being a top-class communicator doesn't imply glib talkers or smooth conversationalists. Effective communicators are people who demonstrate the ability to connect with people through rapport building, listening and showing empathy. They focus on building meaningful and fulfilling connections. Communication is as much about listening, comprehending and responding to what the other person is saying as it is about speaking.

Majority of effective communication in both interpersonal relationships and business involves around analyzing people, listening to them, observing them and calibrating our responses accordingly. For instance, take a skill like negotiation, which is a deep communication subtopic within itself. An ace negotiator is a person who is capable of reading other people like books and modulating their message to pull things in their favor.

Do you know why some businesses fall down the wayside in as little as six months to a year? Because they are solely concerned about making products and pushing them on hapless customers! It's a rinse and repeat the clinical process until customers get fed up and stop buying. Boom, the business shuts down! You can have the most awesome idea in the world or the most ingenious marketing plans anyone can think of. However, if your customers are unable to connect with it, you're heading towards failure.

To be a top class professional or business person, you have to possess the ability to get others to listen to you, while also listening to them and demonstrating understanding or empathy for what they are speaking. This happens when you speak in a way that resonates with people.

As a professional, we are constantly dealing with several external and internal customers. This includes everyone from your managers to employees to potential customers to clients.

The most important aspect of being a seasoned communicator is that it isn't only about you. In fact, effective communication is majorly about your message's recipient. Only talking doesn't automatically guarantee that people will listen. In order to get people to offer you their valuable time, energy and attention, you must be able to pique their curiosity, grab their attention and offer a clear value. They should be able not just to understand you but also be able to relate to you. An effective communicator is someone people *"desire to listen to"* not *"compelled to listen"* (remember that boring in teacher in the class whose sessions we had to sit throughout of no choice?) The sign of a good communicator is someone who people choose to talk or listen to.

If you do not really identify yourself as a person who is capable of holding an unspoken magnetism or charisma over people, mate, you are not the only one. I know plenty of people who are struggling with communication and social anxiety but who've gone ahead and become master communicators owing to sheer determination and regular practice. There are innumerable social awkward people around the world with varying levels of social anxiety. If you are forever worried about people not finding you interesting enough or not being able to say the perfect things at the perfect time, I was there too once upon a time. I know the feeling, and so do several others.

You are gripped by a feeling of being judged every second for not being an engaging conversationalist. You may think people are having a nice laugh behind your back after you've left. I know people who suffer from mild to extreme social anxiety that manifests itself through physiological symptoms such as sweating, excessive anxiety, increased heartbeat, higher palpitations and so on. This isn't to scare you. This is to tell you that social anxiety and the inability to communicate is a real issue.

One of the greatest challenges that people with low social intelligence or ineffective communication skills people grapple with is the ability to connect or relate to others, when communication with a group of people or individual, ineffective communicators get a sense of being out of place! There is a clear feeling of being disconnected and the inability to relate to other people.

On the contrary, those will highly developed social intelligence and communication skills are instantly and effortlessly able to adapt to and connect with people. They seldom have a tough time garnering information about people's feelings and emotion to utilize this invaluable knowledge for forging strong bonds. They are perceptive enough to study other people's communication style and patterns and are seamlessly able to adopt these styles to enable people to relate to them more effectively.

If you identify with the former group, fret not, I have got your back. There are plenty of people sailing in the same boat looking for encouragement, suggestions that work and inspiration, which you'll find plenty in this book.

This book is written to hold your hand and help you go from hesitant or awkward communicator to a superstar communicator in a step by step manner. You won't go from being socially awkward to massively popular overnight. However, you'll take tiny steps in the direction of self-assuredness, confidence, and self-esteem to form wonderful relationships and meet your personal and/or professional goals.

Forming fulfilling personal, professional and social relationships have multiple advantages. You will enjoy a less stressful life, experience more positivity in your surroundings, fulfill your goals, spread joy and inspire people to put in their best, while also increasing your chances of earning more wealth and enjoying the sweet smell of success.

Chapter 1:

Beating Shyness and Social Anxiety Like a

Boss

Let us say, for instance, you want to be a socially confident, self-assured and charming person, who doesn't fear being judged or evaluated by others. When you keep telling yourself that you are a confident, fun, self-assured and charming person, the mind believes it. The thing about our mind (especially the subconscious) is, it doesn't differentiate between reality and aspirations. If you keep saying you want to be a more socially confident person, the subconscious mind believes you are a socially confident person. Thus, it drives your actions in alignment with being a more socially confident person.

A simple shift in your thoughts or the way in which you program your subconscious mind can bring about a huge transformation in your condition. Here are a few proven tips to begin with.

Build a more practical and reasonable image of others

While you idolize others or look up to them, learn to have in your abilities too. Others are also susceptible to the same mistakes and shortcomings that you see in yourself. You really may not know other people's weaknesses or challenges because they may be good at concealing it. This doesn't imply that other people are superior to you or possess greater abilities than you. Everyone is fighting their limitations and challenges, and no one is perfect. Have a realistic view of others. They are humans with a set of strengths and weaknesses, and they falter too. They also make mistakes or go wrong in their judgment. It is highly unrealistic to believe everyone is superior to you or better than you.

Look at times when you've been better than most people. Everyone has their own fears just as you have a fear of social situations. Just because you are afraid of something doesn't mean you should be anxious about it.

Tackle your inhibitions and fears

Rather than brushing your fears and anxieties under the carpet, address. Overcome your social phobia by identifying specific situations that cause your discomfort or duress. Don't avoid or be overwhelmed by them if you truly intend to eliminate these issues.

Avoiding these fears lead to even greater discomfort and phobia, which magnifies the issue. The more we try to escape from something rather than tackling it, the more our condition snowballs into bigger issues. Facing your challenges is the first step towards eliminating them. For example, if a specific social scenario such as public speaking makes you anxious or break out into uncontrollable sweat, rather than fearing it, start facing it. Tell yourself what you stand to lose by not overcoming your fear of public speaking. You will be unable to share your ideas and inputs with others, while also hampering the development of business associations.

Avoidance is a painful cycle that leads to greater avoidance rather than eliminating the issue from its roots. Start gradually by facing yourself in the mirror while speaking. Work on your speech, posture, gestures, expressions and voice tone to look and sound more confident.

Notice how you look and sound. It is really not as bad as you imagine. Slowly, start addressing a couple of friends or family members in a bid to overcome your fear of public speaking. Pick a short presentation or speech that isn't very complicated to communicate. Use the power of non-verbal communication to make your public speaking even more impactful. When you come across as more poised and confident, people invariably look at you in a different light.

Master power positions or postures that make you come across as more authoritative and assertive.

Once you gain a little more confidence, start by addressing a small group of co-workers or acquaintances. Start with easily manageable situations and gradually move on to the tougher ones. Once you accomplish a tiny victory in one process, it is easier to conquer other bigger fears. However, you have to take that one courageous step to begin!

This will not just help you overcome your social anxiety but also boost your self-confidence and self-esteem.

Have more faith in people

Rather than believing that people are always evaluating your negatively, approach them from the point of trust. Understand that people's intentions are not questionable all the time.

You may have had instances in the past where people betrayed your trust. However, attempt to move on from the past by developing greater forgiveness and tolerance. Understand that a few encounters with bad people don't make the world or everyone bad. There are positive and negative people, just like there are sweet and rotten apples.

People may also develop a fear for other people and social relationships when they have been through a damaging relationship or have had their trust shattered. However, with time, effort and consistency, one can start trusting people again.

Here are some tips for building greater trust.

- Be tolerant of other people's mistakes and don't judge them rigidly Find a middle way. Show consideration for what others may have gone through, which has led them to become what they have. Instead of judging people, try to understand them. When you resist the urge to judge people, you gradually get rid of the fear of being judged by other people.

- Stay honest

Speak the truth. Inspire other people's trust by communicating in a genuine manner. Once others trust you, you will find it easier to trust them, and the fear of being judged by them will be gradually eliminated.

- Reach out to people and show them you care by performing acts of empathy and kindness

Don't always place your interests above other people. Be around when people genuinely need you. When people realize you care about their interests as much as yours, they will trust you. Once they develop trust for you, it is easier to trust them.

- Don't seek perfection in people or yourself

Understand that nothing and no one is flawless. Let go of people's weaknesses and limitations while focusing on their strengths.

Take risks to move outside your comfort zone

Even tiny risks that help you step outside your comfort zone and try something that you wouldn't normally do can be beneficial when it comes to beating social anxiety. For example, if you don't normally go for a coffee break with your co-workers and instead prefer sitting on your desk pretending to work, try stepping out for 5-10 minutes during the day. Start eating lunch with your co-workers, even if it is for a short while. It won't transform you from a socially anxious person to a gregarious and confident person. However, you'll take a step in the right direction. Take calculated and healthy risks. For instance, if you are afraid of meeting new people, sign up for a blind date.

Small everyday situations can slowly lead to bigger results. Once you accomplish or overcome small situations, you'll begin to realize that it isn't as bad as you imagine it to be. In fact, you'll end up enjoying yourself or experiencing a warm feeling of relief. This will encourage you to participate in even more challenging social situations.

Instead of being a place that is comfortable and secure (your couch or home), go to the park and make some new friends. Play a sport, cycle or run. Make small changes in your routine where you get the opportunity to meet and interact with new people. Even if it doesn't work out, you'll be happy you gave it a shot.

If you aren't a very confident speaker and always avoid speaking in public, try and proactively volunteer for more speaking opportunities without worrying about how you'll fare. Start with small speaking engagements that aren't very crucial or require you to address a small group.

Take small steps to meet and interact with people who share similar interests and passions. Train your mind to watch out for clues when people want to connect with you. Challenge your thoughts each time they attempt to prevent you from doing something. Each time you find yourself fearing something, start doing it in a small way. You don't have to go and grab the stage directly. Start by opening up to a few people or addressing a small group.

Build your patience, courage, will-power, perseverance

However tough it seems, the only way to eliminate your shyness is to challenge it. It won't happen suddenly or dramatically in a flash of a few moments of enlightenment. It is a demanding process that unfolds in a step by step manner gradually. The idea is not to lose pace.

Each day take a tiny step towards accomplishing your goal of being a more confident and socially relaxed person with courage and patience. Take note of the smallest successes so you can continue the momentum with bigger success stories. Be aware of the fact that just because you suffer from shyness or social anxiety doesn't mean you have to be condemned to a life of loneliness, misery, and isolation.

You can begin being in the company of others and gradually start interacting with them until you are able to face social situations in a more confident manner. Expose yourself to speeches and talks until you are comfortable, you can do the same. Enlist the help of a therapist if required. Tell yourself that a majority of people have more to deal with than evaluate or judge your actions.

Their sole aim in life isn't to mock you or minutely observe every move of yours. When you start thinking on these lines, you will start realizing that people aren't preoccupied with you, which will help you relax a bit.

Even if you falter a few times during the process or eliminate your social anxiety, there's no reason to quit. Like we discussed earlier, it won't happen overnight. It may take several weeks or months to gradually overcome your condition. However, have the patience and perseverance to stick around and so what is required.

Build a more reasonable, practical and balanced picture of yourself

People who suffer from shyness or social awkwardness/anxiety always believe they are inferior to others. They don't value themselves enough or give due importance to their abilities. They don't have sufficient confidence in their abilities or potential.

Start believing yourself by developing a more realistic image. You aren't really inferior to all the people, all the time. You are not unworthy of being loved by other people. Have greater confidence in your abilities and potential. Each time you find yourself undermining your own potential or qualities, think about instances when you did something really well. Don't believe things will go wrong all the time before even getting to the situation. Each time you find yourself indulging in self-criticism, beat it with evidence that proves the contrary.

Think of all the things you do well. Things go wrong sometimes, which doesn't mean they will always go wrong or that you are never going to be enough. Avoid making generalized or sweeping statements such as *"I am really stupid"* You don't have to personalize everything.

Instead of saying *"I am stupid"*, say something like, *"Alright, this didn't exactly go as I thought it would. However, I gave it my best and I am improving with time"*. Take a more realistic approach with your weaknesses and be appreciative of your strengths. For every new challenge you take up, there is a 50 percent chance of succeeding, always remember this. It all depends on your will power and inner strength.

Start by understanding your true and realistic worth, which won't make you feel inferior to others.

Don't seek constant validation from other people about your strengths and abilities. Keep working on your competencies; learn new skills and practice being surer of yourself.

Manage your breath to regulate emotional reactions

Practice breathing and controlling your breath. When you are anxious, you are often short of breath or breathe quickly/rapidly. A quickened pace of breath makes the psychological condition even worse. It may cause anxiety, hot flashes, sweating, and dizziness.

Therefore you eliminate this shyness or physiological, social anxiety symptoms by learning to control your breath. Start by sitting in a peaceful place that is free from distractions. Sit in a comfortable and relaxed posture on a chair or the floor. Focus on your breath. Start counting slowly as you inhale deeply, following by counting while you exhale deeply.

By changing your breathing pattern, you can reverse physical symptoms of anxiety. A small sift in the breathing pattern, rhythm and rate can trigger your parasympathetic response. This is nothing but your body's powerful reaction to Emergency Response, which is referred to as relaxation response.

Concentrate on the breath. Learn to breathe easily while controlling the symptoms of social anxiety or shyness. Each time you find yourself in an uncomfortable position, focus on the breath. When your thoughts wander, acknowledge the stray thoughts rather than fighting them. Get back to your breath gently after acknowledging these distracting thoughts. Allow the fresh air to fill your lungs. Controlling your breath gives you the power to control your thoughts.

Notice how your breath impacts other parts of the body such as mouth, throat, lungs, abdomen, and stomach.

The idea is to be more mindful of the breath by focusing on it to reduce symptoms of social anxiety or shyness.

When you are overcome by anxiety, try mastering the technique by lying down. Later, start breathing in a standing or sitting posture. Break 20 minutes of deep breathing into 4 to 5 shorter relaxation spells that can be practiced anytime during the day.

Avoid self-defeatist, damaging and negative thoughts

People who suffer from social anxiety are often overcome by negative thoughts and feelings, in addition to several prejudices for others and themselves. This worsens their condition.

They will perpetually tell themselves things like, *"I am so stupid or silly"* or *"I am so awkward around people"* or *"I can never say the right thing in front of people"* or *"I am a complete mess around people"*. They think everyone else thinks they are stupid or that their voice starts shaking while conversing with others, especially strangers. There is also a feeling that no one really cares about what they say.

Getting rid of these ideas is critical to the process of recovery. If you want to live a social anxiety-free life, start working towards replacing these self-limiting thoughts with more positive ones. You can either enlist professional help or try to eliminate these thoughts on your own. Identify when and how these automatic negative thoughts make their way inside your mind.

The next time you take an exam or attend a job interview or thrown in a social situation, stop thinking about things that can go wrong. Question your own negative thinking patterns. *"Am I certain other people think of me as incompetent or inadequate? Is there any evidence that they hold a negative opinion about me?"* Try to reframe your thoughts by giving them a more positive or realistic twist. Avoid catastrophizing thoughts or thinking in extreme terms. The more realistic and rational truth is things aren't as bad as you imagine them to be. When someone doesn't answer your call, it may not be because they are avoiding you or don't like you. They may be busy in a meeting or driving to work.

Shyness or social anxiety originates from a deep-rooted need to imagine the worst. You always imagine people don't like you or think you are stupid or perceive you in a highly negative manner. The realistic truth is often far from it. People aren't always evaluating your appearance (unless you are a reality star or actor) or judging your conversation skills. It is just your tendency to blow things out of proportion that leads to having such self-damaging thoughts. The reality is more balanced and somewhere between black and white.

Each time you find the monster of negative self-talk showing up in your head, talk back to it. When you talk to your inner critic, you take away its power to control your mind and actions. Telling the critic you don't want to listen to what it says makes it powerless. Start to speak and order the critic to vanish. Tell it that you refuse to listen to it or believe it. Tell it that its lies have been called out on many occasions. Make the inner critic aware of the fact that you are demonstrating greater kindness towards yourself, where it has no place.

One strategy that works wonderfully well when it comes to beating negative thoughts is to give your critic a name. Then have an ally with another name. Each time 'Bunny' feels the urge to tell you how miserable you are, let 'Peter' intervene and talk about how well you did at the event you last attended. Allow the ally to offer as much evidence as possible to contradict everything the critic says.

Make daily reflection a habit

You hold limitless potential within you that simply needs to be unlocked! Take time out to reflect upon who you are and what you are capable of accomplishing. It will help restore a sense of balance and coherence in your life. Establish a higher sense of purpose and peace that will make your life more meaningful.

Set aside a few hours of your day for self-reflection. Ask yourself questions such as, what is my true potential? What are my positive traits, skills, and strengths? How can I contribute to make other people's lives more meaningful? What am I capable of accomplishing that I haven't yet accomplished?

Surrender yourself to these reflections to make your life more meaningful and purposeful. It will allow you to focus on the positive instead of negatives.

Journaling, visualizations, affirmations, and meditation are all powerful tools of self-reflection. In journaling, you write your thoughts in free-flowing consciousness without thinking too much or censoring them. You write thoughts as they come to your mind while attempting to give them a more positive direction. In the process, you are programming your subconscious mind into being a more self-confident and self-assured person who is at ease in social situations.

You start writing what you want to accomplish or your goals for yourself. When you constantly write about what you want to accomplish, you are tricking your subconscious mind into believing it as the truth. The subconscious mind is unable to differentiate between imagination and reality, and hence directs your actions in alignment with what it believes to be real.

Write about your goals, desires, and objectives related to social anxiety. Ensure that you read these goals periodically to keep reminding yourself about them.

For example, if you keep writing that you are a confident, self-assured individual; your mind believes it to be true and directs your body to act in a manner that reveals greater confidence and self-assuredness in social situations.

Think about instances during the day when you revealed greater self-confidence or overcame your fear for people or make a small attempt to face the situation rather than fleeing. It is best to write a journal before going to bed because when your conscious mind is resting, the subconscious mind is in its element. When you think these thoughts just before sleeping, you are allowing your subconscious mind to process and absorb the information.

Our mind has a constant stream of involuntary thoughts running through it. The pace is so rapid and undetectable that it becomes difficult to single out distinct thoughts. It's pretty much like the background music you hear while you are working. Though you aren't actively focusing on it, it is there somewhere. We don't even notice our thoughts, yet they impact us on multiple levels.

Just like background music impacts your mood, emotions, and state of mind without you even noticing it, our thoughts have the power to shape our behavior without us realizing it. The involuntary self-talk going on in the mind can shape your reality in a more positive way if you can reprogram your mind consciously with more constructive thoughts. Instead of allowing your self-talk to remain in the background, bring it to the forefront and use it to program your mind in a more positive way to inspire positive actions that help you beat social anxiety.

Affirmations are positive statements that attempt to condition your mind towards believing positive and hopeful thoughts, thus leading to more positive actions. Repetition is the key to programming your subconscious mind. When you keep repeating a thought over and over again, your mind is tuned to perceive it as your reality. Thus, it guides your actions in sync with this reality. Here are some affirmations for people suffering from social anxiety.

Affirmations must always include positive words, must be repeated several times during the day and must be said in the present tense as if it is already happening. Also, avoid using negative words in affirmations. For instance, if you want to say, *"I am not socially shy or awkward"*, say, *"I am socially confident and effortless"*.

Replace negative words and phrases with more positive terms. This way, you are not confusing your subconscious mind, which doesn't understand negative terms. By saying, *"I am not shy or socially awkward"*, you are only reinforcing shy and socially awkward, the exact opposite of what you wish to accomplish.

Similarly, meditation is another powerful self-reflection tool. Pick a meditation style that best suits your purpose. Sit in a relaxed posture and start by focusing on the breath. Gradually, get into a deeper state of consciousness by paying attention to your thoughts and body. Focus on each part of the body and feel the energy within it. Feel a fresh lease of energy, positivity, and hope within each part of the body.

Start from the head and move gradually downwards until you reach the feet.

Focus on positive reflections, and watch out for your thoughts, feelings, and words to avoid being swept away by negative thoughts. When you find yourself overcome by negative, destructive or self-damaging thoughts, simply acknowledge them and move back to the positive thoughts and feelings.

I personally find visualizations very effective when it comes to overcoming shyness and social anxiety. When you imagine certain visuals, you are again sending powerful signals to the subconscious mind. Our mind is highly receptive to visual symbols and often absorbs them more effectively than words.

Shy and socially anxious people tend to over focus on the idea that people are paying attention to them or judging them all the time. No, everyone's eyes are not on you all the time. Operating with the thought that all eyes are on them and therefore they should speak and act in a specific way only intensifies the social anxiety.

When you visualize yourself as being a part of any social situation will trigger feelings of anxiety, shyness or nervousness. However, if you visualize the same situation from the point of standing out among the crowd, you'll feel more at ease. Don't immediately imagine yourself giving a presentation to the audience. Rather, visualize yourself as the audience to reduce anxiety.

Visualize yourself as a smart, self-assured and self-confident person. Close your eyes and relax completely. Turn on soothing music and imagine yourself in a social situation. Visualize each detail. How do you conduct yourself in the setting? Visualize yourself as a well-dressed, confident and popular person who is communicating with people effectively. Pay close attention to details such as your attire, body language, mannerisms, speech, walk, voice, expressions, and posture.

How do you greet new people? How do other people perceive you? What are others saying to you? Think in terms of sensory experiences. What do you hear, see, smell, taste and feel? Involve as many senses as you can within the visualization. Practice visualization for a few minutes every day (preferably before going to bed or first thing after rising). You will gradually begin noticing the changes it will be about in your persona. You are feeding powerful symbols to the subconscious mind, which will slowly align your actions with these thoughts.

If you are afraid of attending an upcoming gathering or event, simply visualize it before actually attending it. Visualize the situation in detail. Visualize yourself as a friendly, uninhibited and confident person who is relaxed in the company of others. Imagine how people around you are acting, reach out to you and socializing with ease. The subconscious mind will gradually start connecting these images to real life situations, which will reflect in your attitude. When people observe your attitude, they will respond to you more positively.

Visualization is known to be one of the most powerful tools when it comes to fighting shyness, social anxiety, and social phobia. Use it in combination with other techniques for optimal results. For instance, you can combine affirmations, journaling and visualizations to gradually overcome social anxiety.

Identify problems and fears, along with their triggers

By focusing on your problems and fears, you are actively looking to eliminate elements that are making your fear or existence even worse.

For instance, if your partner or another family member is constantly judging, criticizing or making uncharitable remarks about you, there are high chances it can worsen your self-esteem and thus make you even more fearful of social situations. Similarly, if co-workers are constantly making unflattering remarks about you, it can lead to an even greater frustration and social anxiety situation.

By focusing on your problems, you are able to identify triggers that are furthering harming your condition. It gives you the opportunity to focus on a solution – to surround yourself with more positive and inspiring people in your life who lift you instead of breaking you apart. If something or someone is augmenting your fear of being judged negatively by others, look for ways to avoid the person or situation. By identifying things that make matters worse, you can focus on solutions.

Chapter 2:

Overcoming Lack of Confidence and the Fear of Being Judged

If there is one thing that hampers the process of effective communication and prevents us from being our natural, confident and self-assured selves, it is an ever-looming fear of being judged by others. This is especially true of people who are shy or suffer from varying levels of social anxiety. They are perpetually functioning with a mindset that each time they speak or perform any action; the other person/people are judging them or secretly mocking them. The need to avoid leaving behind a negative impression is so compelling that they stop interacting with people altogether.

People can put themselves through highly self-defeating behavior to avoid the possibility of being judged negatively by other people. For starters, you may elude telling others what you truly desire to tell them. You may avoid speaking at work, parties or class for fear of 'not being good enough' or ridiculed. You may not tell your loved one your real desires, or you may hesitate to ask your manager for a raise. You may not want to tell a new date where you prefer to take them for dinner. The hesitation is arising as a result of fearing other people's judgment can impact all areas of your life and prevent you from enjoying more rewarding relationships by sharing authentic/genuine ideas, feelings, viewpoints, and emotions. You'll stop being yourself and try to be someone you are not just to please the other person or to avoid being judged by them.

The fear of judgment is deeply connected with the inherent need to be liked and accepted all the time. This can be psychologically rooted in our childhood and early adolescent experience. The need to be liked and accepted by others is so powerful that it stops us from communicating in an uninhibited manner. Thus we are unable to express our true selves in the process. It is a fact that human beings are forever judging each other. They are always forming impressions about whether they like or dislike something or whether something is good or bad. Then, there are plenty of layers in between the two extremes. As we keep processing new information, our mind is assessing and reassessing things, which is a continuous process.

Rather than avoiding an issue by not mentioning anything about our opinions, feelings or preferences, and working in the direction of pleasing everyone all the time, try to overcome your own fear of being judged by people. Accept that the fear exists, and actively work on this fear or anxiety to tackle the bull by its horns.

Owing to this fear, they are unable to make meaningful conversations, engage in healthy discussions and enjoy fulfilling relationships with people. Are you someone who finds it excruciatingly painful to communicate with people for fear of being judged by others? If yes, you aren't alone. Here are some tips on overcoming this fear to facilitate more open, effective and fearless communication.

Judgments are unavoidable

Even the best and most successful people in the world are judged. Therefore, there is no escaping it. Resist the urge to control or influence other people's judgment about you. It will affect the way you communicate with them. There is only so much you can do to control other people's judgment about you. Don't demand that other people shouldn't judge you. It doesn't help to expect that we should be able to live without being judged unless you live in a rabbit hole. People have a tendency to judge other people words, actions, decisions, values, behavior patterns, beliefs, attitude, and ideologies. They may or not may express it, but they'll judge. It is a more physiological human brain process, where we take in information and process it using our own filters of biases, attitudes, beliefs, ideologies, prejudices and so on. It is almost an uncontrollable and involuntary process.

While communicating, make it easier for people to avoid judging you by sharing the context of your feelings. This will make it easier for people you are sharing the information with to understand you with the required understanding and compassion. Compassion is the ultimate judgment killer. Think of it is judgment's very own kryptonite. The two can rarely co-exist. When compassion, understanding, and sensitivity are around, judgments have little power. Context offers people the opportunity to understand your situation with greater empathy by placing themselves in your shoes. Thus, there is no tendency to judge you.

For instance, if you are telling someone that your relationship is almost ruined because your partner is constantly at the receiving end of your suspicions, also offer some background information or context to help them view things from your perspective. In the above example, the listener is likely to judge you as an over possessive, jealous or suspicious partner. However, if you mention that you've been cheated and lied to in past relationships, which feeds your fear of being cheated in the current relationship, the person may understand you more effectively. Give people enough information to help them see things from your perspective and avoid making sweeping judgments based on stray facts here and there.

Bring about a shift in your perception

One way to beat the fear of being judged is to bring about a clear shift in your perspective in the company of other people. Divert focus on another aspect instead of emphasizing on what and how other people are thinking about you. Try to focus on conversations while also attempting to be in sync with other people. Understand that much as you'd like to focus on who or what you are, people do not focus on it.

Even if you say something awkward or your actions are embarrassing in your opinion, people barely notice them. We may obsess about a small thing we may have said to someone weeks ago, and unrealistically expect that the person is still holding on to it pretty much like us. There are high chances the individual has completely forgotten about it and moved on to other things. Their memories aren't as powerful as you imagine it to be.

During the process of communicating with people, if you experience the fear of being judged by others, find something to focus on soon. A majority of times, the fear of being judged isn't as apparent to the other person as we think. Focus on some sensory experiences connected to the event to shift attention from what the other person is thinking about you or how he/she is judging you. How do your surroundings look, smell and feel? What type of sounds do you hear? Is there music playing in the background? How does the food being served taste? This is especially true in social situations where we are always anxious about being misjudged by people we are meeting for the first time.

This will help divert your attention from the fear symptoms to having a good time by interacting in a friendly and meaningful manner with the other person. Lets us assume you are a corporate networking event. Here, everyone is nervous about making a favorable first impression. Similarly, during a recruitment interview, all potential candidates are jittery about making a favorable first impression and eventually being hired by the organization.

Understand that irrespective of the situation you are in, almost everyone is sailing in one boat. This makes it easier for you to deal with your fear of being judged in certain situations.

Identify your strengths and weaknesses

When you know your inherent strengths or are confident about what you are great at, you are less likely to bother about what others think about you. The tendency to be affected by other people's judgments is far less when we are confident and aware of our own capabilities. Be self-assured about your strengths and know your shortcomings better than others. If someone forms an opinion or judgment about you, they are forming that judgment based on their filters, which may not have much to do with your own abilities.

When you are aware of your abilities or strengths, other people's judgments will wield less of an impact on your during the process of communication. While talking to people, be aware of your own strengths, personality characteristics, and vulnerabilities. This way, the impression others form about you will not hold much relevance for you. You will continue saying what you have to in staying true with your own nature. Do not allow others to kill your individuality, personality, and character based on their judgments about you.

When you don't believe in or stand for something, you will tend to believe everything. Similarly, when you don't have a clear understanding of your own personality, strengths, and attributes, you will believe whatever others think about you. Lack of confidence or self-awareness is the biggest catalyst for being affected by other people's judgments. Take stock of your own strengths and weaknesses while communicating with people to avoid going with whatever they want you to believe about yourself. Assume charge of how you view yourself if you want others to view you positively.

Everything is temporary

You will rarely fear judgments if you realize that nothing about these judgments or what people think about is permanent. The thing about the human brain is, it has the capacity to process limited data. Though we make innumerable judgments, they don't' have a place in the memory bank forever. However much you believe otherwise, people are not going to remember that one awkward moment of yours forever or every time they meet you. There is only so much information one can practically retain in the realms of the brain and conscious memory.

When people make certain judgments or impressions about, there are high chances that a few days or even moments later that judgment may have left their conscious awareness. Our understanding of people is not made based on the tiny setbacks, awkwardness or mistakes in what they say or do. For all you know that one moment you thought you were really awkward and people will remember it for a lifetime, they may forget about it before saying goodbye to you after the first meeting.

Though an overall impression about people is quickly formed when we meet them (remember the first four seconds rule?), our understanding of others is not based on their minor behavior patterns or words. It is more dependent on a pattern of the schema of big things that others say and do. There is a pattern in the manner with which they interact with us and make us feel over a period of time. This is how we form an impression or judgment about them. If the overall pattern of your words, actions, and behavior with other people are positive and favorable, they will not form negative judgments about you based on one stray moment, a wrong word used here and there or an awkward action.

The human brain considers a larger perspective in a broader schema of things. Thus judgments, opinions, and perspectives change over a period of time. It isn't now and never, however scary it may appear to be. You may not have a second chance to make a first impression, but during the course of your interaction with the person, you do have an opportunity to establish a pattern.

You are not being judged all the while

Keep in mind that this looming fear of being judged by people every time exists in your mind and isn't real. This is a more extreme and unrealistic type of thinking that leads us to believe that we are being judged all the time. A more balanced and real perspective is – no one really gives a damn! Honestly, people are more preoccupied (especially if they are meeting you for the first time) with how other people perceive them than forming opinions about others. Believe it; people are as nervous about interacting with you for the first time as you are. A majority of our social phobia or anxiety originates from the notion that we are being judged all the time. That's far from reality or rational thinking;

People have more on their plate then judging you. This fear of being held under the microscope for every word and action will prevent you from communicating with others in a meaningful and rewarding manner.

Bear in mind that others don't always make you the center of their focus during the process of communication. They are more often than not thinking about what to say or do next instead of forming an opinion about you. Even when people think about it, they rarely think about you in the manner in which you think about yourself. Try to analyze people's thoughts while communicating with them. What are they implying through their verbal and non-verbal communication patterns? They seldom perceive you in the same negative light that you perceive yourself. Take advantage of multiple social contexts to shift your negative or self-defeatist thoughts. Stop the cycle of negative thinking in its tracks by performing a physical action (thinking biting your tongue or pinching yourself) to snap yourself out of the thought process.

Once you realize your negative thinking is impeding the process of communication, get back to communicating naturally and uninhibitedly with people. Adopt a more neutral communication process if you find it challenging to make it overtly positive.

Practice challenging your thoughts by thinking of evidence that is contrary to what you believe. Is there solid proof that you make a complete fool of yourself every time you talk or interact with people? Is there glaring evidence pointing to the direction that people don't like to talk to you or are disinterested in you every single time? Keep thinking on evidence to the contrary when you find yourself being bogged down by negative thoughts.

Bear in mind that to a certain extent, everyone is anxious while communicating, especially if they are meeting you for the first time. At some level, all people struggle with some fear or anxiety of being judged. Understanding this can help you realize that no one's judging, ridiculing or criticizing you all the time. They are in fact dealing with their own fears, uncertainties, and insecurities, far from being obsessed with judging, seizing you up or criticizing you at the level you imagine.

Beating the fear of being judged while communicating needs effort and practice and cannot be overcome in a single day! Develop new thoughts, behavior patterns, ideas, social skills, and more.

Preparation is the key

The more prepared you are while communicating with people, the lower will be your tendency to experiencing jitters about what other people think about you. We saw in the earlier chapter on small talk about how you can stay up to date with the day's latest stories or know more about a person before meeting them. Similarly, if you have a presentation or discussion, study all facts ahead to support your explanations and arguments. The more prepared you are while communicating with people; the lower will be your fear of being judged negatively by them.

We are more confident, self-assured and in control of our words and actions when we know what we are doing. The more we prepare, the more confident we are while approaching and conversing with people. Keep all facts, figures, and numbers handy. Have genuine interest to understand people's desires, preferences, likes, interests and so on. Listen to them carefully to understand what the other person is trying to convey through both verbal and non-verbal communication.

Practice and preparation reduce your fear of being judged. One of the best ways to conquer your fear of being judged during the communication process is to observe how you appear and feel while communicating. What are your typical expressions, gestures, movements, posture and so on while talking to people? How do appear while interacting with other people in varied situations? Stand facing a mirror, and pretend to talk to people, address an audience or make a presentation. How do you look and feel? Do you feel more confident when you realize you don't appear as bad as you think you do? Does facing yourself in the mirror increase your confidence and sense of self-worth?

If you are going for an interview, practice answering in a perfectly calm, poised and confident manner. If you are approaching people at a business networking event, practice talking in a more approachable, open, welcoming and friendly way. Keep preparing and practicing multiple communication scenarios before the mirror until you no longer experience the fear of being judged. Even in the event that people come out guns and daggers after you, it may not take long for you to take them on in a more solid, confident and well-prepared manner. Being confident also awards you the strength to conquer the fear of being judged.

Keenly consider your own judgments

There's seldom a more effective way to stop being bothered by other people's judgments than to stop judging yourself and other people. At times, our fears are imaginary. People who suffer from social anxiety almost always believe that everyone is judging them. This fear is far from realistic or balanced. Watch your own thoughts, ideas, language and perception about yourself. What words do you use while describing yourself? How do you view your own words, actions, and behavior? Do you see your own actions or behavior patterns in a positive or negative light?

Obvious, sometimes judgments are unavoidable. If a person has been terribly rude or means to you, you aren't going to think they are angels incarnated. However, watch the words used in your head for certain people, behavior patterns and events. Reframe the focus on your own judgments. Rather than saying, *"someone sucks"* or *"someone is a total loser"*, question yourself about the effect that person has over you, which you may want to avoid or gain awareness of in future.

For instance, *"He has never followed through with his commitments made to me"* or *"She tells me she's doing her best but ends up disappointing me"*. Don't label people; instead, identify what they do to have a certain impact over you. Resist the urge to classify people as good or bad character. Instead, communicate in a manner that is healthy for you. If a certain behavior pattern on someone's part has an unhealthy effect on you, learn to identify its impact and deal with it instead of labeling people.

Watch the most common words you use for yourself. If you are constantly referring to yourself as *"loser"* or *"failure"*, you are as guilty of judging yourself as others. The biggest barrier to the process of communication is our tendency to judge ourselves.

That little nagging voice in our head needs to be silenced more than anyone else. People will have countless opinions, notions, and ideas about you. They are entitled to their thoughts, and it isn't much you can do about it. This is an important step when it comes to overcoming the fear of being judged by people. If you are forever bogged down by what others are thinking about you during the process of communication, take stock of your own confidence, self-esteem, and sense of self-worth.

Identify how your inner critic addresses, and any negative thoughts that it ignites within you that hamper you from relating to other people. If your inner critic is constantly telling you that you are a fool when it comes to trusting people owing to a few bad experiences, you will not be able to trust people while conversing with them. Your beliefs and negative comments about yourself will lay the ground for your communication with other people, so watch what you say to yourself.

Know how much you contribute to the fear of being judged during the process of communication. What role does the filter of your own negative thoughts play when it comes to your fear of being judged? Take control of your actions, thoughts, and beliefs to start making small shifts in your perspective or thought process. Stay positive and optimistic instead of worrying about what others think about you.

Chapter 3:

Secrets of Small Talk and Conversation Building No One Will Tell You

Now that we've tackled shyness/anxiety and the ever-looming fear of being judged in social situations, let us move on to another effective communication and rapport building secret – small talk and breaking the ice with strangers in social situations. Why is small-talk so vital when it comes to mastering social skills?

Small talk can, indeed create big magic when it comes to wowing people and building lasting relationships. There is something about people who have mastered small talk. They are charming, irresistible and possess the knack of sweeping people off their feet instantly. This magnetism and charisma help them climb dizzy heights of popularity. Have you ever noticed how some people almost always manage to be crowd pullers at every party or event? These are the glib talkers who make people feel comfortable and engrossed in a conversation.

All of us know someone who slays it when it comes to connecting with others or building a favorable rapport. The person knows precisely what to say and how to say it for creating the desired effect. How do they manage to capture people's attention every single time? Small talk or making conversation is not an inborn trait. It is something the person has mastered over a period of time, and you can too! They make it seem effortless and smooth. It seems like these savvy conversationalists can never say anything wrong.

What is this secret for being an incredible people magnet that small talk experts have mastered and others do not know? Trust me; there's no magic wand or genie involved. There are high chances these people have painstakingly studied and conquered the art of building a rapport with others through the power of small talk. Small talk can be huge when it comes to building a favorable rapport with people and connecting at a deeper or more subconscious level.

A study has revealed when we meet someone for the first time; it takes the person only 4 seconds to build an impression about us, which largely stays the same throughout our future interactions with them. Think about it; you have only 4 seconds to make a positive impression on people. Sounds scary? The idea is to give people a sense of belongingness and affiliation, to make them feel comfortable in your company and to make the first interaction memorable.

Studies at Michigan University have demonstrated that small talk and thoughtful interactions increase our problem-solving mechanisms. Constructive and meaningful communication comprises getting a hold of other people's thoughts and trying to look at things from their perspective. This is vital when it comes to considering a problem from different angles and coming to a solution. It helps people develop strategic thinking, problem-solving skills, and lateral thinking.

Did you think about why some people are almost always successful when it comes to making friends, grabbing complimentary drinks at the bar, making unforgettable conversation and generally sweeping others off their feet? The answer is simple words is – small talk. It is indeed critical when it comes to making a favorable first impression and getting them interested in interacting with you more often.

Yes, small talk seems like a mammoth task to some people. They break into a sweat when it comes to approaching strangers or initiating a conversation with unknown people. The ice-breaking gives them jitters, and they believe they will make a complete fool of themselves. The fact remains that you don't have much time to create a first impression, and whatever you say or do can break or make that crucial initial interaction. Small talk is indeed the foundation of every fulfilling and rewarding personal, social and professional association. We form mutually rewarding and beneficial relationships on the basis of a favorable first impression or connection establishing small-talk.

The objective of small talk is to show the other person how interesting, well-informed and credible you are as an individual. It is also related to rapport building, creating a common ground to feel a sense of oneness or belongingness with the other person and for supporting future interactions.

By engaging in small talk, you can successfully determine if the people are indeed worthy of associating with you in future for building more meaningful, rewarding and beneficial social, professional and personal associations. At times, causal small-talk can lead to lasting relationships with folks who are similar to you or in a similar situation as you.

Bedazzle people by building a positive first impression using these incredibly helpful small talk rules.

Mirroring

If there is one powerful tip that has existed since primordial times for building rapport and feeling a sense of oneness with a person, it is mirroring. It is the key that helps us establish a positive rapport with other people at a subconscious level. Mirroring has been in place throughout evolution and is still one of the best ways to get people to like you or feel that you are 'one among them.' The human brain is wired to identify people who are similar to them. We are invariably drawn or attracted to people who appear to be similar to us. There is an instant connection with people who are similar to us or like us at a highly subconscious level.

The best way to make a person feel that you are similar to at a deeper, subconscious level without them even noticing it is to simply mirror their actions, words, gestures and so on. If you are on a mission to build a favorable impression on someone you have just met, mirror their actions, gestures, movements, voice, choice of words and posture. Carefully notice their non-verbal and verbal signals, and mirror it for creating feeling belongingness, likeability, and familiarity.

An expert tip is to keep your mirroring actions subtle and discreet to avoid giving the other person the impression that you are mimicking them. Use this technique for leading people to think that you are just 'one among them' or like them. This not just increases your likeability factor but also helps build a favorable rapport with anyone.

All you have to do is smartly identify the most words or phrases used by the person and drop them subtly while talking to them. For instance, if you find someone calling their business as their *"empire"*, use the same word when you refer to their business. What happens when you do this? On a highly subconscious level, this increases your chances of getting the person to not just like you or feel a sense of oneness with you but also relate to you on a deeper plane, thus leading to a glowing first impression.

Bear in mind that the mirroring should look natural, subtle and effortless. It shouldn't appear forced or like you ate trying to make a huge effort to get into someone's good books. Avoid looking nervous about identifying and aping every action or gesture the person makes. This will defeat the entire purpose of this strategy. This not just boosts your appeal but also facilitates the process of helping people bond with you more efficiently. People will respond and relate to you more favorably when you pitch yourself as a person who they are able to identify with.

Avoid discussing unknown, unfamiliar or complex topics

It can be awesome to have a discussion about space science with a space researcher or scientist. However, it is always safe to go with subjects you are comfortable discussing or familiar with. This gives you the much-needed confidence when it comes to making a favorable first impression on people. Why talk about known topics? You are already running low on confidence and slightly inhibited by the prospect of meeting new people or not saying the right things. If you start venturing into unfamiliar terrain, it will lower your confidence even more. The person you are interacting will have a certain edge over you, which will nosedive your confidence levels, while also making your ignorance obvious. This can lead to an unflattering first impression. You will rarely recover from saying something dumb or sounding downright stupid, thus impacting the entire conversation. It is nice to talk about varied topics but avoid picking topics that make you appear clueless and ill-informed. Throwing half baked details just to impress people makes you come across as pretentious and fake. An expert can easily call your bluff if you don't know what you are saying.

When someone is talking about a topic that you don't know anything about, avoid bluffing your way simply to gain attention. Rather, employ self-deprecating humor to genuinely admit something such as, *"All I know about space is the one that exists between my bedroom and refrigerator"* if you know nothing about space research or science while talking to someone who is deeply interested in these topics or a professional. Isn't it better to be appreciated for your humor than be the butt of all jokes for your lack of knowledge or ignorance? You'll appear more genuine, realistic, natural and confident when you can laugh at your own shortcomings. Learn to convert weaknesses into strengths. Lack of knowledge can be cleverly utilized for making yourself look more genuine, honest, less mechanical, more relatable and entertaining.

Do not be shy about helping people enjoy a good laugh at your expense; you will not just appear more honest and less fake but also discard the opportunity for other people to laugh at you or take a dig at your shortcomings. It'll increase your confidence by several levels. People are more blown away by witty and self-assured people who possess the confidence to admit to their weaknesses than fake folks who attempt to demonstrate their foolishness by sharing half-baked information.

Use open-ended questions

We've discussed this earlier in the active listening chapter. It works like a charm when it comes to making small talk and getting to know people. Getting someone to open up about themselves is quite an art, and the secret is to ask more open-ended questions. This will not just allow the other person to open up about themselves but also helps you identify a common ground for enjoying a memorable conversation. Avoid making it a one-way communication. In fact, start by offering some interesting information about yourself and then ask the other person. Don't play FBI asking lots of open-ended questions without sharing information about yourself.

Try to maintain a balance between sharing something of your own and subtly getting the other person to talk by asking open-ended queries to get to know them. It'll be a more interesting balanced conversation and appear less intrusive or interrogative. For instance, let us say someone is excited about an upcoming games season in the city. You can begin the conversation for talking about it. You can ask the person why they support a specific team or what makes them want to join a particular team.

Here are some examples. Person 1 – Have you heard about the season's upcoming games in xyz city? Person 2 – Oh yes, everyone is stoked about it. I am cheering for team ABC, what about you? Person 1 –Oh, I am supporting team IJK Person 2 –

what makes you support IJK? Person 1 – They have a strong defense, and I am also a huge fan of player G. Person 2- Oh yes, that's right. Have you played the game ever? Person 1 – Oh yes, I used to play for the varsity and the local city team as well for many years before quitting owing a back injury. Person 2 – This is impressive; can you share your winning strategies, please?

So here someone has started the conversation, and as Person 2, you are simply building upon it. You get the drift, right? The objective is to create conversation by giving some details about yourself and asking people questions to ensure a more freely and smoothly flowing conversation or information exchange.

Effective conversationalists are expert in recognizing other's interests, key drivers, emotional hot buttons and passions. They know exactly what drives people, and how to steer the talk in the right direction. These communicators pin down people's emotional hot buttons and make the conversation sticker by talking about things that the other person is interested in or can relate to. If you listen to seasoned conversationalists, you'll understand that they are savvy people who are adept at identifying the other person's interests pretty early during the interaction. Not just that, they'll also build upon it until the other person is passionately engaged and involved in the conversation.

Let us say, for example, you realize that a person is an avid traveler and adventure buff. This valuable information can be harnessed in several ways for rapport building. You can begin by talking about your own travel and adventure sports activities while urging them to share their most memorable trips and adventure memories. You can speak about your experiences with different cultures and regions. Ask them about their most memorable vacation. Or a funny travel story. This is one way of making room for an engaging conversation that keeps people enthralled and hooked.

Stay abreast with the day's news before going for a gathering or networking event

This is one of the best tips when it comes to conquering small talk like a boss. Before attending an important gathering, networking event or party, stay abreast with the day's latest news, events, and happenings. It helps to stay well-informed and up to date with what is happening around you while making small talk. This makes you come across as an intelligent, interesting and articulate person. Just before you head towards the vent, dedicate a few minutes for browsing through the day's important news stories. Use this for creating a *"conversation starter bank"*. You have all the matter you need to initiate an engaging conversation instead of being at a loss of words or not knowing where to begin. You can simply start with any one of the ready topics and open the door for an interesting, meaningful and memorable conversation.

Ensure that you do not go after controversial topics related to politics, international conflict, and debatable global affairs. Instead opt for relatively safe subjects such as a breakthrough in medical or technological research, new scientific trends and so on, where there is little scope for the difference in opinion. You don't want to start World War 3 in a ballroom, do you? When you keep a conversation bank ready, it ensures there aren't any awkward minutes of silence or pointless fillers. This helps you keep other people completely hooked to the talk!

Maintain a balance between asking questions and making statements

Small talk should be a nice balance of statements and questions. If you pose too many questions, you may come across as intrusive and probing. Similarly, if you go on and on by making too many statements, the other person will not have an opportunity to speak!

Keep the interaction more balanced, relevant and meaningful by mixing statements and questions. Begin by making some statement and include a question at the tail end. For instance, *"I genuinely enjoyed ABC television series although plenty of people thought it was it over hyped. What is your opinion about it?"* You are offering your opinion, while also giving the other person a chance to express their take.

Go with universal, non-controversial and neutral subjects

When you are talking to someone for the first time or initial few times, as a thumb rule, go with more neural, evergreen and universal topics. Don't pick culturally, religiously and politically sensitive topics where people can have diverse views. This is even truer when you are talking to people from diverse nationalities, cultures, races and so on. What are some safe and evergreen topics? Environment, movies, local city, health, and medical research, technology, weather, books, science and so on. Avoid talking about war, political ideologies, religious differences, terrorism, and global conflicts.

Try to figure out common ground and stick to it throughout the conversation. For example, if you realize that the person you are interacting with is an avid foodie, go with topics such as new eateries in town, popular city regional foods, international delicacies, and other similar food-related topics. Then again, if you realize that someone is a big sports fan, talk about weekend games, best places for games buffs to go to within and around town and winning game strategies. I am willing to bet my last cent people will be all charged to make an enthusiastic, spirited and engaging conversation.

Many luxury vehicle salespersons are actually trained to identify their potential customer's interest so that they can build upon it to strike a favorable rapport. For example, if they come across gym equipment or gear in the vehicle, the salespeople will start talking about their cardio training sessions or weight training routine. They will offer muscle building tips or discuss healthy eating. The aim of this strategy is to boost the salesperson's likeability, build a positive rapport, leave behind a stellar first impression on the prospective customer, which boosts their chances of selling to a potential customer.

Disagree in a healthy and respectful manner

While making small talk, you may not agree with everything the other person says. However, learn to disagree in a healthy, balanced and respectful manner without getting offensive, aggressive and confrontational. This will damage your chances of creating a positive impression on the other person. Use a more diplomatic and genuine approach such as, *"This is a novel, different and interesting way of looking at it or considering things. I never thought about it this way. Can you elaborate?"* Now, this approach will keep things pleasant while still showing disagreement. A potentially volatile situation can quickly turn into one of constructive and healthy discussion. Learn to spot potentially negative conversations and quickly change them into pleasant interactions by using a more balanced approach, where you can make your point without offending the other person. Being assertive without coming across as aggressive in your interactions is the key to be an ultra-effective communicator. Aggression is, *"I am always right and you are always wrong"*, while assertiveness is, *"I have the right to be my view and so do you. Let us agree to disagree without changing our views"*.

Ask for suggestions, recommendations, and advice

This is my absolute favorite when it comes to acing the 'small talk creates big wonders game.' One of the best ways to help people feel a sense of belonging, similarity, and affiliation with you is to show them feel important (we've discussed this briefly in above). Oscar Wilde famously said, *"We admire the wisdom of people who come to us for advice"*. People will automatically believe you are impressive, smart and have great discretion if you approach them for suggestions, guidance, advice, and assistance. Don't you appreciate the wisdom and good sense of people who come to you for advice, opinion or suggestions? Use this inherent human tendency to establish a favorable rapport and facilitate the process of communication. When you approach a person for advice or suggestions, they will not just feel wonderful about themselves but also view you are someone who possesses great taste.

People normally love speaking about themselves unless they have a more reticent or reserved persona. They are most comfortable while talking about their experiences, expertise, passions, and knowledge. You'll get them all charged and pumped up if you ask them for suggestions related to their area of passion or expertise. Research has demonstrated that talking about ourselves helps us feel great and stimulates the same hormones that are activated when we make love or eat delicious food. Now that you know the secret to making inroads into a person's consciousness by leaving behind a positive impression, use it to the hilt. Keep learning new things or gaining interesting insights from other people. They will have no option but to find you an irresistible communicator. When you are stuck for topics to talk about, simply ask people for suggestions and opinions.

Always remember people names

Have you read Dale Carnegie's communication and social relationships bible *How to Win Friends and Influence People?* One of the best strategies mentioned in the book when it comes to leaving a favorable impression on people is remembering their name and using it many times throughout the interaction. In many social situations, when we are introduced to people, there are rapid introductions, where lots of names are shared, and unknown faces are to be remembered. It can be a challenge to recall everyone's names. When so many details are exchanged, you may not remember these names later. Use this as an advantage and pick up as many names as you can by mindfully listening to people when they share their names. When you take people's names in the interaction, they'll be mighty impressed you remember it.

Get into the habit of memorizing everyone's names. One technique is to repeat it after being introduced to the person. For instance, *"Hi, I am Joe"*. *"Hey Joe, where do you work?"* or *"Hey Joe, nice to connect with you here"* or *"Hey Joe, are you also Sam's friend?"* Keep repeating their name naturally until you commit it to your long-term memory. However, don't sound stupid by repeating over and over like a stuck record. Taking names should appear to be subtle and natural.

Don't we all feel special, wonderful and valued when someone addressed you with your name? It adds a more intimate and personal touch to the interaction. Doesn't it offer you a wonderful sense of importance when you realize that someone managed to remember your name despite being introduced to several people? Doesn't it make the communication more appear more connection-worthy when someone addresses you by your name? Avoid feeling awkward about addressing people using their names even if they have only been introduced to you.

Using someone's name makes you appear more likable, irresistible and relatable. If you didn't catch someone's name, it is fine to gently ask them to repeat it rather than addressing them using an incorrect name.

Have the discussion or talk focus on the other person

Top conversationalists understand that small talk and building a glowing impression on others is centering the interaction around them. Make others the epicenter of your conversations rather than focusing on yourself. However, if you get a feeling that the other person isn't comfortable with the spotlight shining on them or he/she appears socially awkward, shift your focus from them till they begin feeling comfortable to open up.

Few people enjoy listening to folks who only talk about themselves, and their accomplishments, talents, positions and so on. Of course, you are impressed but it gets boring after a while. I mean, there's only so much you can hear about other people. There isn't any need to explain your life in excruciating detail to strangers, including what your neighbor's dog ate for breakfast. Big no-no! Focus on others. This makes appear less self-centric, self-assured and likable.

Use greater *"You"* than *"I"* statements through the conversation. This will help people understand you are keen on knowing more about then instead of yapping nineteen to the dozen about yourself. Show that you are genuinely interested in other people. Listen to them attentively and mindfully by observing verbal as well as non-verbal clues. This makes you come across as irresistible.

Include personal stories, anecdotes, experiences and metaphors

Charismatic communicators know how to sweep listeners off their feet by sharing likable, relatable and interesting personal experiences and anecdotes. They make every interaction or conversation memorable by sharing stories from their life or revealing to the other person how they have been in a similar situation. It makes these people appear more relatable, likable and identifiable. This strategy also helps create a foundation for building more meaningful relationships.

Sir Paul McCartney utilized this strategy brilliantly when it came to be developing a rapport with the performance before each live performance. The musician would go about offering a background story or inspiration behind a particular song or share a fascinating behind the scene anecdote or incident while the song was being created. This added greater charm to his performance. Another wonder tip for being an ace conversationalist is to utilize rhetorical questions generously throughout the interaction. Are you having a wonderful time? Do you know this powerful secret related to ABC? It keeps the listener totally hooked to what you are saying by building anticipation.

One power-packed tip followed by effective communicators is using contrast for communicating their ideas in a more persuasive manner. For example, statements like, *"we are concerned about the value we provide to our customers"* can be delivered in a more compelling way by using the element of contrast along the lines of, *"While our competitors and other companies focus on low prices, we concentrate on offering greater value to our customers"*. The contrast makes what you are attempting to express, appear more power-packed, thus leaving the other person thinking.

Metaphors are another powerful arsenal in n effective communicator's bag. They make for effective conversation elements since they stimulate the listener's sense of imagination, and form more vivid imagery of what he/she is attempting to convey. As a speaker or communicator, you can stir the perfect feelings, imagery, and emotions in people by employing metaphors. Keep a few metaphors ready for common topics of conversation, situations, and ideas. Go online and find metaphors for some of the most common and complicated topics. As a communicator, you can make your point more compelling when you are able to help your listener understand complex topics by using simple, everyday metaphors.

Do some research groundwork

I know someone who is an incredible social magnet and has folks eating out of his hands. One of the most awesome tips I've learned by observing him is finding interesting little details about someone's background just before meeting them. It's like a piece of quick background information, which isn't really tough in the digital age. This technique may not always be possible. However, if you know the name of the person you will be meeting, it helps to do some background research.

When you are aware that you are going to meet ABC or a group for the first time, do some digging to gather information. This will help you build a more rewarding and meaningful interaction with the person.

For example, let us say you are attending some social gathering, where you know you will find plenty of musically inclined folks. You know the gathering will make have people with a specific interest or passion. Thus, you can dig deep into knowing more about various musical forms, latest chartbusters and more. This will help you come across to date and, well-informed, likable and exciting about a topic that is of interest to plenty of people.

Recognize things that echo with people in the group or gathering and use this valuable information to enjoy stimulating conversations with them. Folks you have just met will completely hook into what you are saying because they are passionate about the topic. At times, enjoy playing Sherlock Holmes and looking for clues about what a drives a person through their social footprints. Don't being a virtual stalker. It's just some harmless digging around for knowing more about the person, so you know what to talk to them when you meet them. Go through the person's profile on social networks for understanding their background, profession, interests and so on. You'll gain a good idea of people's personality to connect with them using favorite spots, teams, interests, television series, likes, preferences and more for keeping people enthralled throughout the conversation.

Know more about people before meeting them to give yourself a clear edge over others when it comes to rapport building. However, guard against being judgmental or holding preconceived notions about people before meeting them. The idea is to facilitate communication, not hamper it. Keep an open mind while knowing more about people and approaching them.

Develop superior listening skills

Communication is a two-way process that involves talking and listening. It isn't merely about revealing your superior listening skills but also about practicing active listening by plugging into what other people are saying.

Speaking is integral to the communication process. However, if you don't keenly listen to people, you will find it challenging to connect with them or adapting to their communication style, communication needs, emotions, personality, and intentions and so on. A superstar conversationalist is not someone who can talk until their jaw hurts. It is also about knowing where people come from and appropriately responding to what they say. Make others feel relaxed, open and comfortable in your presence.

When you want to sweep people off their feet and leave behind a dazzling impression, offer them complete attention when they are talking. Your body language should be more responsive and open and less rigid. Avoid crossing your legs and arms and tilt your head slightly in the person's direction when you are addressing them. Keep your feet firmly pointed towards the speaker. Subconsciously, it tells the other person that you interested in what they are saying and not looking to escape from there.

Give plenty of verbal as well as non-verbal acknowledgments to demonstrate that you are listening to people. For example, nod your head, say *"aha"* or *"I know how you feel"*. Ask meaningful questions or paraphrase what the other person said to show your interest in what they are saying. People need acknowledgments that you are listening to them if you want them to open up.

Avoid sharing increasingly personal/intimate details while engaging in small-talk

This should be a given, but it is amazing how many people manage to break this unsaid small-talk communication rule. While some folks take time to open up, other people are quick in recounting the last several decades of their life in 10 minutes. There is no need to open up about everything in a bid to establish a favorable rapport with strangers. Doesn't it drive you nuts when people launch into an autobiographical mode, sharing the most intimate details about their lives with someone they barely know? Spare people painful details about your troubled childhood or rebellious teens!

However, I know small talk and communication experts always suggest sharing some details about yourself to break the ice and establish a favorable rapport with the other person. The middle way is to share enough interesting tidbits to what the other person's appetite or pique their curiosity but not veer in the territory of the intimate details.

Share interesting pieces of information about yourself without appearing weird freaky. Hold back the urge to share intimate, personal or confidential information during small-talk. Remember, the person is still a stranger until you get to know them well. Everyone doesn't have the same threshold when it comes to sharing personal details. Some people may not be comfortable talking about their personal life or hearing about yours.

Also, you face the risk of this information being misused by the other person. Another big no-no is gossiping or bad-mouthing others (especially common friends or people known to both you and the other person). It depicts a pathetic picture of you as a person. You will come across as someone who cannot be trusted to retain other people's secrets or a person who is constantly talking behind the backs of other people.

No conversation clues? Scan your surroundings

At times, when you don't know what to say or are stuck for clues (your biggest fear maybe the conversation coming to a dead end), the best strategy is to look at your environment for clues. It can be anything from a tune playing in the background to wall art to something someone is wearing or even a brochure lying around. There are clues everywhere, which you can pick up to start a stimulating conversation. All you need to do is observe your surroundings carefully. Keep an eye around you to kick-start an engaging and interesting discussion. How do you know if a person wants to talk about a topic? Again, observe how they react to what you've just said, and then determine your next course of action. For example, when you talk about the long line at the buffet table, what is the other person's reaction? Does he/she look like they want to speak more about it, or do they simply smile and shrug it off?

One thing to keep in mind while using this small talk and communication technique is to pick topics that are positive, appropriate for the occasion or person and relevant. Avoid talking about irrelevant and inappropriate topics that border on gossip or negativity. The other person will end up garnering an unflattering impression about you. Feel-good topics are the best when it comes to enjoying a memorable and engrossing conversation.

If you are new to a city, you can ask locals for suggestions about places to visit or dine at. People instantly take to those who ask them for advice and suggestions because it gives them a sense of importance. In a way, you place them on a pedestal and make them feel valued. They will end up thinking you are smart (since you asked them) and feel an instant subconscious connection with you.

You'll open an entire box of topics by soliciting suggestions from people. It will start an engaging conversation about a variety of things, including city, culture, arts, music, food, attractions, sports, communities and more. It's like unlocking a treasure chest of conversation goodies! Few people dislike talking about the place they grew up or live in.

When seasoned conversationalists don't know too many people at a social or business gathering, they will use connection builders such as, *"How do you know the hosts, Michael and Angela?"* This gives us a platform to identify a common ground for starting a meaningful conversation.

The 20-second rule

If you are stuck between how much to speak and how much to listen during your small talk sessions, stick to Dr. Mark Goulstan's 20-second rule from a book he's written called, *Just Listen*. Mark doles out a practical, realistic and actionable solution that can be compared to following traffic rules. This is how it goes – during the first 20 seconds of speaking, you are operating on a green light. The listener will actively listen to you only if you make appropriate, engaging and relatable statements. You have 20 seconds to pique their interest and get them to listen to you.

It is very rare to be able to hold people's attention beyond the initial 20 seconds. Only a few gifted conversationalists are able to accomplish this. Very few people are able to hold someone's attention while they are speaking for more than 30 seconds without appearing boring or chatty. The subsequent 20-second window is when your yellow light begins. You have now gone beyond the limit. After 40 seconds, you are in the red-light window. Stop in your tracks right here and don't go any further. I know you are not going to keep looking at your watch while conversing with people. However, a quick glance should help you figure out the duration of your talking time. The urge to continue can be overpowering. However, if you are approaching 40 seconds, wind up quickly. Give the other person a chance to speak.

Once you give the other person sufficient time to speak, get back to talking if the person is still interested in listening to you. Try and keep your talking and listening time equally. This creates a good balance when you are communicating with someone. Both you and the other person feel heard.

Killer conversation starters

You will never have a dearth of conversations if you master these clever and engaging conversation starters. I know and empathize with people who get stuck while approaching new people because they don't know what to say or how to make the conversation more interesting. When you are at a loss of words, and the conversation faces the prospect of reaching a dead-end, here are some ways to revive it.

1. Where are you originally from? Is it far from where you currently live? How is the weather in your native city? How is life back in your hometown in comparison with the current place of residence? If given an option, would you continue living in your native town/city or your current place of residence? Get people to talk about their birthplace to create a warm and fuzzy feeling and make the conversation more memorable.

People almost always associate their birthplace with positive feelings, and the same feel-good factor they experience during the conversation can help subconsciously transfer these feelings to you. This association is exactly what plays out when we experience certain feelings about hearing some songs. There are high chances we heard the song during a particular time in our life when we were undergoing certain emotions or experiences, which is why playing the song or piece of music evokes the same emotions in us. Similarly, talking to people about a positive, fuzzy or feel-good topic will facilitate the rapport building process and boost your likeability factor.

2. What are the top three items sitting on your bucket list currently? What are your travel plans for the current year (if the person mentions travel as one of their passions or hobbies)? Which places have you been to? Which is your favorite holiday memory? Which is your favorite holiday destination? There are plenty of questions you can ask about a person's passions, interests, and hobbies to build conversation effectively.

3. Which television or Netflix series are you currently hooked on to? Why do you enjoy watching it? Which television series or movie comes closest to your life? If offered a choice to live in the setting of your favorite book or television series, which would you pick? The idea is to get the other person to open up and engage in an interesting conversation.

4. Which is the latest movie or television series you've watched? What did you like or dislike most about it? Do you recommend it? Is it worthy of all the hype it has generated?

5. You remind me of a celebrity but can't figure out whom. Which well-known person do people generally compare you to?

6. Which was the last concert you attended? How was the entire experience? Which is your favorite musical band? What kind of music do you like listening to?

7. Why did you choose to be in this professional or opt to work in a specific sector? Did you aspire to be here from the beginning? Were you always interested in being (their profession)? How did you develop a passion for working in this

sector? Would you recommend this choice of career to your children or other aspiring professionals?

8. Hey, how do you know Jane and Joseph, the hosts? How did you hear about this gathering or event? How did you join the Federation? In short, you are asking the other person rather politely how they landed up there. Any questions that pertain to their presence, there can be good icebreakers to kick start a memorable conversation.

9. What is the highlight of your day? What do you like doing in your free time? Which is your favorite sports team? What are your hobbies, interests, skills, and passion?

10. Which are some of the city's best places to hang out? Which attractions, eateries, parks, cafes, museums and so on are worth visiting in the city?
These are just a warm up to get you started with the conversation. Keep building on the conversation to make it more interesting and engaging.

Chapter 4:

How to Use Voice, Speech, and Language for Being a Pro Communicator and Influencer

Don't you wish to be a super influential and effective communicator who has people eating out of your hands? In an earlier chapter, we discussed the finer nuances of conversation and how it can help us break the ice while sweeping people off their feet. This chapter is dedicated to exploring how we can effectively use the power of speech, language and voice skills to boost our charisma and confidence for being an effective communicator.

Are you expressing yourself in a positive, compelling and confident manner? Are you an articulate and engaging communicator? Are you expressive and confident when it comes you addressing an audience? A powerful communicator possesses several attributes, which can be mastered over a period of time. While non-verbal communication is integral to the process of being an effective communicator, we focus primarily on verbal communication in this chapter. What are the elements of an amazing conversation or speech? It comprises several characteristics such as intonation, tone, inflection, words and much more to lend greater meaning and clarity to your message for helping you communicate articulately.

Here are some power-packed tips for boosting your language skills to come across as an interesting, persuasive and effective communicator.

Maintain an even paced and steady rate of speech

Your rate of speech is the speed with which you speak.
Have you observed how some people speak so fast that you can barely grab what they are trying to communicate? Similarly, some people speak so slowly that you are bored to death until they finish speaking. If you want to be an effective communicator, maintain a steady, consistent and well-paced rate of speech. It should neither be too fast nor too slow. People who speak very fast, often come across as anxious, nervous, emotional, dramatic and dominating. Similarly, when you

speak too slowly, you come across as inhibited, indecisive and confused. The listener may soon switch off either way when they cannot effectively process what you are trying to communicate.

The middle path is to talk neither too fast nor too slow. Keep a balanced and steady rate of speech of around 140-160 words per minute. Time yourself while you speak at your normal pace and check your rate of speech. If you go above 160 words per minute, buddy people are going to have a tough time keeping up with what you are saying. Make it easy for your listeners to process what you are saying by keeping a uniform rate of speech.

When you make a very important or substantial point, where you want the idea to sink into your listener's consciousness or make them think for a while, pause after saying it, this will create the desired effect. Give them time to process the magnitude of your message by staying silent for a while. Allow whatever you've said to sink in as intended.

Develop an articulate and extensive vocabulary

An articulate, clear and expressive communicator is someone who knows how to talk about feelings effortlessly, ideas, concepts, experiences and so on. To be able to create a vivid picture in people's minds, one has to be able to express themselves using the most appropriate and interesting words and phrases. You have to use the exact expressions to make yourself more attention-worthy and relevant.

Keep working on building an extensive vocabulary to boost your self-assuredness, poise, and charisma during social and other scenarios. Commit to learning three-four new words or phrases each day. People with extensive vocabulary rarely face any trouble when it comes to expressing their views and demonstrate higher confidence levels while speaking to people. There is something irresistible about people who are always using the right words at the right time. Think about it like this – the difference between a functional and extensive vocabulary can be the difference between a dazzlingly colorful and black and white image. Painting pictures with words is an art that makes the conversation even more stimulating and gripping.

Emphasize on the correct word to communicate the intended message

The word you emphasize on makes all the difference when it comes to conveying a message clearly. Let us consider a sentence like, *"Did he steal my book?"* Now, let's look at how emphasizing each word can keep changing the message. If the speaker emphasizes *"he"*, it means the speaker is asking if *"he"* stole the book or someone else did it. Similarly, he/she emphasizes *"steal"*, the speaker is implying that he/she is unsure whether someone stole their book or simply borrowed it. The again emphasizing on *"my"* conveys the speaker isn't certain whether someone stole their book or someone else's. Finally, emphasizing on *"book"* conveys the speaker is implying he/she doesn't know if his/her book was stolen or something else was stolen. Get the idea? The word you emphasize on while speaking conveys the meaning you intend to convey. Emphasizing on the wrong word can completely change the meaning of the sentence.

Keep away from redundancy

Avoid loading your conversation with too many fillers. Keep sentences crisp, pithy and to the point. Avoid using highfalutin terms to showcase your vocabulary. Instead, use the most relevant, effective and widely understood term. Use appropriate words and phrases to communicate your ideas in the most effective manner. Less is more when it comes to vocabulary. A gifted speaker or communicator is someone who manages to convey maximum ideas using minimum words or phrases.

Think of more effective and articulate ways to communicate your ideas and feelings. Try replacing everyday words and phrases with punchier or more compelling terms. For instance, instead of using *"very hungry"*, you can say *"famished"*. Similarly, *"very angry"* can be replaced with *"livid"*. Get the drift? Again, to become a more effective speaker, try to eliminate redundant terms from your everyday conversations. For instance, *"they said (whatever they said) about my new dress"* can be replaced with *"they commented on my new dress"*. The objective is to make your speech more expressive, crisper and compelling. Focus on making your sentences tighter by replacing ineffective words and phrases with more relevant expressions. Everyday words such as *"big"* or *"large"* can be replaced with *"colossal"* or *"gigantic"* Likewise, sacred can get a makeover with *"petrified"* or *"spooked"*. Get into a pattern of consciously thinking up better ways to say something. This habit will increase your impact as a communicator. It will make you come across as an interesting, arresting and colorful conversationalist. Build a richer vocabulary to lend greater character, feelings and sensory experiences to the conversation.

How do you go about it? Use a small pocket diary or notebook for writing down new words and phrases you tend to come across every day. Try to include these words and phrases on everyday usage. Master three to four random words from the dictionary each day and try to use it in your conversation. There are tons of 'word a day' apps on your smartphones to keep your vocabulary more enriching. It is a work in progress. You will never completely master the vocabulary game, but you'll keep getting better. If you are one of those people who believe that a limited vocabulary prevents you from holding a conversation, think again. Breathe easy. There are many multiple ways to build a powerful vocabulary if you have the will to do it.

Utilize inflection in speech effectively

There are several ways to pack more punch into your conversation. One such valuable tip is to use inflection for optimal communication efficiency. Inflection or intonation pumps more value into your communication. Avoid communicating in a sing-song tone if you want the listen/listeners to take you seriously.

Vary your tone periodically to avoid coming across like a robot. Effective communicators seldom use a monotone while speaking. They keep playing with or varying their tone to suit their message. Intonation instills greater feeling and emotion in your speech. It facilitates the process of communication by conveying exactly what the speaker wants. Through a person's intonation, you will know whether the person is being requested, urging, commanding, questioning, suggesting, patronizing and so on. This eliminates the process of miscommunication.

Many times, faulty inflection leads to miscommunication. For instance, let's assume, you wish to request someone to do you a favor. Rather than slightly elevating the tone towards the end of the sentence, if you maintain a flat tone, the request will sound more like an order or command. A slight rise in the inflection towards the end of the sentence will make it appear like a request. The listener may get the idea that they don't have the option of refusing you if you are making a statement instead of politely requesting them. This is a classic case of miscommunication. Therefore, using the appropriate inflection and intonation is critical to the process of communication.

Make a conscious effort to get more variety, character, and clarity into your tone if you want to come across as a persuasive and engaging communicator. Intonation brings a wider range of emotions, ideas, and character into your communication. Sometimes, even some amount of inflection can alter the meaning of the entire message. A simple suggestion runs the risk of coming across as condescending. Other times, our tone can make all the difference in changing the meaning of a message. Our a tone, as well as inflection, are the most common causes when it comes to creating misunderstandings in the process of communication.

Be mindful of the tone and pitch you use while talking to people. There are three main pitches that can be used in normal conversation or speech. The three fundamental pitches are high, mid and low speech. As a compelling communicator, utilize varied pitches. Play with your voice to communicate your true feelings and intentions as required.

The best way to know how your sound is either record your voice while speaking and hearing it later or standing before a mirror while talking. Narrate a detailed account or story while focusing on how you look and sound. This helps enhance your speech delivery. Identify areas that can be worked upon to make your speech or conversation more power-packed. Without rehearsing, try to talk about any random topic for a couple of minutes. You will know the exact through of your voice, while also gauging the desired effect of your sound. Once you know your weak communication spots, it is easier to work upon it.

Keep in mind that your voice is your biggest weapon as a communicator. Use it generously to your advantage to convey your ideas in the most effective manner. Avoid speaking in a monotone, especially when you are delivering an important speech or engaging in an interesting conversation. Our voice can be one of the most flexible communication tools, which can be used by adding plenty of effects, feelings, and coloration. It will add more punch to your communication.

If you want to make an important point, begin on a flat note. Then, elevate your pitch slightly towards the middle, and end it on a flat note again. Avoid ending what you are saying on the high pitch because this makes your statement come close to a question. Ensure you end on a flat note, so it seems like you are making a strong statement rather than raising a question. As someone who wants to master communication, you can also enlist the services of a voice and speech coach to make your presentation and conversation skills even stronger. Use a lot of variations to add more variety to the speech.

Keep your pronunciations and enunciations clear

Start working on your sound articulations to come across as an effective and compelling communicator. Have an impressive command over phonetics for sounding good and reducing the chances for misunderstandings. Your sounds and appropriation should come across as intended.

Avoid mumbling, muttering and speaking under your breath if you want to be an effective speaker. It takes away from delivering the message in a powerful manner. Few things are as unflattering as people whose speech is barely audible. You will have to keep saying the same things over and over again, leading to confusion. Open your mouth loud, wide and clear while speaking to drive home the message effectively. This will lend more clarity to what you are saying. Aspirate your sounds correctly to sound good. Aspiration of sounds is vital where speech clarity is concerned. Understand when you are required to stretch or condense a sound. One letter or a group of similar letters can be utilized for creating multiple sounds that one should be aware of while talking or giving a speech.

For instance, take *"beat"* and *"bit"*. While the former has a longer *"I"* sound, the later is shorter. Then again *"pull"* and *"pool"* are aspirated and pronounced differently even when both communicate similar sounds. When unsure, go through word pronunciations online or use an app to check the correct sounds.

Even the same letters are aspirated distinctly using varied words and phrases. For example, *"the"* used in *"thick"* has is even more aspirated than *"the"* sound in a word like *"they"* or *"the"*. Likewise, *"day"* and *"they"* are articulated distinctly even though they sound close. For those experiencing difficulty with enunciating or articulating sounds, try mouth exercises for increasing your jaw flexibility. Use tongue twisters to master varied sounds enunciations and articulations.

Chapter 5:

Breaking Free from the Loop of Negative Communication Patterns

Being an effective communicator and social being is also about avoiding negative communication patterns. We now know only too well how vital and indispensable effective communication and social skills are within our daily personal, business and social life.

Great communication skills aren't just needed by political leaders and orators, but anyone who desires to enjoy rewarding and fulfilling relationships. You need it for everything from negotiating a lucrative business deal to persuading your partner to dine at your favorite restaurant. Yet we falter with social and communication skills that should come naturally to us. Miscommunication leads to misunderstandings, arguments, and breakdown in relationships.

Let us consider a situation where, as a project leader, you are attempting to explain to a team member where they've gone wrong with the project. You have said all that you had to, simply to realize that the person is not listening. He/she has mentally switched off as is evident through their mannerisms and body language. Think about your boos overacting to a tiny issue, which you obviously can't tell him/her for fear of the consequences.

There are tons of such awkward communication scenarios where we make mistakes that break our connection with people or fail to convey a message as desired. The worst part about these communication errors is that we can't even identify where we've erred. We fail to realize why a person didn't react in the intended manner or the reason we couldn't get someone to do what we wanted them to or why they have stopped listening to us. Then, these tiny misunderstandings grow into bigger issues until you find it impossible to communicate with the other person.

Here are some of the most common communication mistakes or negative communication patterns and strategies to overcome them to make you an effective communicator and help you enjoy more rewarding relationships

The mind readers

This is another negative communication pattern or stumbling block when it comes to effective communication. Before you finish speaking your sentence, the person will jump in and complete it for you. They claim to know and understand exactly what you want to say even before you say it. This makes them ineffective communicators because rather than actively listening to what the speaker is trying to convey, they act on the assumption that they already know everything. This makes them switch off. This tendency to think *"I know what he/she is going to say"* or *"how he/she feels"* prevents us from actively listening to people, which means we can end up losing plenty of important information.

Listen keenly to each word people speak, tune in to their voice and observe their body language to comprehend their message in the right context. Avoid reading clues in isolation. For instance, if a person is fidgety, it can be a sign of nervousness, excitement or a hyperactive persona. Look at everything from their body language to choose your words to their voice. Avoid singling out isolated information pieces from their verbal or non-verbal communication and make sweeping conclusions based on it to assume you have understood them. This is one of the biggest communication blunders. Understand the message as a whole by being a mindful listener without sweeping judgments, assumptions and conclusions.

We are all guilty of selective listening, which can be a huge hindrance to the process of communication. Instead of listening to what the speaker intends to communicate, we hear only what we want to and lend it our own interpretation. For instance, when someone says, *"I want you to ace this"*, the person may mean that they want you to excel at something. However, you may interpret it as, *"you suck at this currently"*. This is nowhere close to what the speaker implied. The intention behind what they said was completely different from the way you interpreted it. The speaker implied that they wanted you to boost your competency levels to accomplish stellar results, which is not the same as you are lousy at it right now. It only means there is plenty of room for improvements. However, with your filters, you only hear what you want, which proves a hindrance to the process of effective listening. Avoid filtering what people say or pick up a few words/phrases here and there.

Rather, pay keen attention to what the speaker is saying and try to gather their message as a whole, complete with all verbal and non-verbal clues to be a more effective communicator.

Let us consider an example of selective listening for understanding how it can negatively affect the communication process. Susan had a particularly stressful day at a restaurant where she worked as a waitress. She gets home after a busy night and finds her husband Samuel glued to his favorite television series. He casually inquires how her day was, and the much stressed Susan mentions everything that went wrong that evening. To begin with, the place was packed with customers, so she had to deal with a lot of crowds. Later, she did not manage to get a lot of tips that evening. Susan finishes off her rant by saying that though she served a group of customers, who ran up a huge bill of $500 particularly well by going out of the way, they didn't tip her. She was frustrated and upset that people could be so inconsiderate.

Samuel didn't speak much and instead broke into laughter. Susan asked him where he found humor in the entire situation when she was clearly upset. Samuel mentions the laughter wasn't in response to what she said, but at the hilarious situation on the show, he was watching.

Susan started losing it by now. Samuel didn't say anything to comfort or reassure Susan, which made her question Samuel if he had even heard what she said. *"Of course I heard everything you said, you should be glad you made a tip of $500 from your last table for the evening"*. Susan, livid by now, picked up her things and marched out angrily, slamming the door. Samuel was bewildered about her reaction. What wrong did he say to elicit such a negative response from her? Do you notice the problem in their communication? Samuel practiced selective listening. He was not actively listening to Susan when she was pouring her heart about how bad her day was. He only caught bits and pieces of what she was saying while focusing his attention on other things, much to her angst and disappointment.

Even when you commit to completely hearing the person out, your life can be full of instances where you unknowingly practice selective listening. We hear only what we want to while eliminating important information from the communication, which hampers the entire process. It may come across as highly inconsiderate, insensitive, stupid, rude or disrespectful to the speaker. Make an effort to listen to and interpret the speaker's message in its entirety.

Obsessed with hijacking and winning conversations

The most negative people to deal with during any communication process are probably the ones who are obsessed with winning every discussion, argument, and debate. They believe it is their birthright to hijack or win every discussion. Read it as many times as you like but you are never ever going to win any argument or get people to agree with you by starting your discussion with, *"I am going to prove you wrong now"* or *"I am going to prove this point to you now"*. You will simply end up raising the person's defenses by stating straight off the bat how you are hell-bent on proving them wrong.

While communicating with people (especially when it comes to debates, differences, and arguments), do not fan the other person's defenses. The listener is likelier to prepare for a mental battle ahead if you inform them that you are on a mission to prove them wrong. Plenty of people make the mistake of saying, *"That is not true. Let me prove how incorrect you are"*. What is the whole idea about informing someone that you are going to prove them wrong? Go about proving your point in a more logical, balanced and thoughtful manner. Keep in mind that changing someone's mind, perceptions or views is never going to be easy. When you establish fairly early that you want to prove something to someone, they will rarely listen to you or admit that they are wrong or that you've managed to prove yourself right.

Avoid letting others know that you are going to prove them wrong. Do it cleverly using facts and reasoning. Even if you know the listener is clearly wrong, play along and say something to the effect of, *"Well I was thinking slightly differently regarding this, and I could very well be wrong. I am frequently wrong, much like everyone else. Let us look at the facts now, should we?"* Notice what we did there? We adopted a more neutral, balanced, logical and scientific approach, which is tough to contest. It drops the other listener's defenses.

No logical person on earth will disagree or object to something like. *"I can be incorrect. Let us consider the facts"*. What would be a scientists' approach? Do they go about trying to prove everyone wrong? Or are they only concerned with uncovering facts? Your communication approach during arguments and differences should be the same – sticking to facts. Using a balanced and scientific approach while dealing with potentially uncomfortable subjects or arguments can make you an effective communicator!

We rarely get into trouble for admitting we can be wrong too. It prevents the issue from escalating and automatically causes the other person to assume a balanced approach too at a subconscious level. They will also adopt a balanced, logical and fair stance when they find you demonstrating greater objectivity. The listener will realize that they could be wrong, too, just like you. When you attack, the other listener follows the same pattern at a subconscious level. When you bring down your defenses by mentioning you could be wrong, the other person is likely to follow suit. Don't tell someone they are wrong right at the beginning if you really want to prove them wrong.

When people do not face strong emotions or resistance, they are likelier to alter their stance. On the other hand, when people are told they are wrong, they don't just resent it but strive harder to prove themselves right. This leads to a never-ending loop of arguments, ego battles, conflicts, one-upmanship and much more. When people get the feeling that their knowledge, views, beliefs, sense of self-worth and values are under threat, their stand toughens. An effective communicator knows how to make people drop their guard and be more open and flexible by mentioning upfront that they (the speaker) could be wrong.

Avoid playing Mr./Ms. Fix-It all the time

When someone is speaking to you or pouring your heart out to you, unless they actively solicit advice or suggestions, resist the urge to offer solutions or fix things for them. Many times when people share their struggles, challenges, feelings or emotions, they aren't looking for solutions. They may probably know that something cannot be resolved, which is exactly why they are so rattled by it. All they need is someone to lend them an empathetic ear.

Overcome the desire to offer unwanted suggestions, however compelling the urge if you want people to take you seriously or talk to you. Listen to the speaker attentively without chiming in with your two cents. Sometimes, only acknowledgment and empathy can completely change the way they are feeling.

Let us look at the conversation. Person A, *"The baby is has given me sleepless nights. I have barely slept in the last week. It is tiring, stressful and exhausting"*.

Person B, *"You should consider supplementing breastfeeding with bottle feed, so the little one doesn't get too hungry every now and then, especially at night. When it sleeps on a full stomach, it won't keep waking you hungry"*.

Person A didn't necessarily ask Person B for a solution, but Person B out of well-meaning concern nevertheless suggested what can be done to overcome a challenging situation faced by Person A. Many times our suggestions and are well-intended and offered out of consideration for the other person. However, it can still backfire if all the person wants is to be heard. Compare this with something like, *"I really understand how stressful and tiring handling a newborn can be. It can sap one's energy completely.*

However, you are indeed doing a wonderful job, and this is merely a phase that passes once the little ones grow up. Then, you'll miss these days. Once the kids grow up and live their independent life, you'll remember these days fondly". See what we did here? We acknowledged Person A's feelings, comforted them, encouraged them, appreciated their efforts, and urged that they make the most of these moments. Won't this make the other person feel better instead of offering practical, clinical advice?

Neutralizing messages

Notice how several leaders and communicators render themselves ineffective when they neutralize their message by following a powerful thought or message with fluff. The message is stripped of its impact. The person begins by saying something compelling. This is followed by pondering about its impact, which then leads the speaker to finish with fluff. For instance, you may say something like, *"Honestly, I didn't mean to say you are ineffective but..."* or *"I didn't really mean to be rude or anything*". It robs the message from its efficiency. You may not be able to communicate what you are trying to with the desired impact.

Neutralizing messages can also occur in the form of non-verbal gestures like smiling, diminishing your posture, shrugging and more. It may not be conspicuous; however, it decreases the effect of your message at a deeper, subconscious level. Effective communicators avoid resorting to neutralizing messages. They will communicate their message in a non-offensive manner without killing the impact of their message. They will communicate their message without sugar coating it and listen to the other person's response.

Likewise, stay away from using one size for all approach while communicating with different personalities. Every person has their own distinct personality, fears, desires, views, communication needs, and expectations. Ascertain that your communication adapts to or adjusts to these differences whenever possible. For instance, you may be teaching a group of people with different personalities and learning styles of their own. Consider these differences in personalities and learning styles to make the learning as effective as possible. Some folks may benefit from a more theoretical learning approach, while other people may prefer a practical and hands-on mode of learning. An impactful communicator is someone who can consider different learning and communication styles to make sure they are understood.

The seasoned defendants

The defense person is someone who stops listening and starts attacking in the middle of the conversation by defending themselves or their actions. Each time someone says something that sounds critical, we raise our defenses. We think people are attempting to pull us down even they are offering constructive and well-meaning criticism. Likewise, if you are communicating with a person who stops listening and begins defending themselves, make your criticism sound non-accusatory. This will get the person to listen more keenly and consider your point of view.

Drop the listener's defenses by utilizing the sandwich technique by adding a potentially critical or negative statement between two positive statements. Let us consider an example of the sandwich method. *"I think you are an awesome dancer; your form, style, and movement are impressively varied. However, I would be really glad if you can work on facial expressions to achieve the same degree of perfection. You will be one of the most skilled dancers in the group if you do it"*.

Did you observe what we did here? We juxtaposed a potentially negative or offensive statement (that the dancer is not very good with facial expressions) between two feel-good statements to make it more palatable for the listener. The listener is likelier to lower their defenses and accept your suggestions. The method can be successfully used across personal, professional and social relationships.

Every time you intend to discuss a potentially uncomfortable or negative topic with someone, avoid saying it straight off the bat. The person is likelier to react negatively or defensively since they are caught off guard. Instead, offer indicators and signposts. We've had all seen street signposts that give us clues about directions to our destination. Give people a heads-up about what to expect. Mentally prepare them for what is coming next instead of just dropping the bomb. Begin by saying something such as, *"I genuinely want to resolve this issue else I wouldn't be speaking to you about it"* or *"I could do with some reassurance or comfort from you which is exactly why I am discussing this with you"*. You are giving the person the required importance by mentioning that if the problem or issue wasn't important for you, you wouldn't have brought it up with the person.

You are talking about the issue simply because it is important for you. You are making your point in a non-offensive or non-accusatory manner. The listener is likelier to think that the objective of your communication isn't to accuse or blame them but seek reassurance from them, which will make them less defensive and more open to the idea of listening to you.

If you don't want people to get defensive or launch into an argument, don't make your statement as if it is the ultimate truth. Start by mentioning you can be wrong, and that both you and the listener should consider or evaluate facts to determine if you are right. Mention up front that there is a possibility you could be wrong. This helps the other person drop their guard instantly. They will be more open, approachable and receptive to your view.

Rather than giving the other person the feeling that they are responsible for everything for what you are feeling, take responsibility for your feelings by utilizing more "*I*" and less "*you*" sentences. This makes you appear responsible for feeling something, much like it is your point of view and no fact. It will sound less accusatory or offensive to the listener. They won't get a feeling that you are criticizing or accusing them of something, which brings down their defensiveness.

Rather than telling the listener, "*you rarely have time for me*" or "*we don't spend enough time together*", you can make it more digestible and acceptable for the listener by saying something such as, "*I'd really like if we could spend more time together because I cherish our moments together*". In the latter statements, you are communicating your point without blaming the other person. It conveys your needs without accusing the other person of being inconsiderate towards your feelings. In a way, you are accepting responsibility for thinking or feeling in a particular way.

People stop listening to us when they feel like you are attacking them. Let us say a project leader has to convey to his/her team that they are not efficient where a particular project is concerned. Rather than saying, *"You are not working efficiently or being productive on this project"* or *"This team is ineffective, and now you do things the way I ask you to"* say, *"I possess vast experience in managing projects of this nature and the way forward to be more effective is this ..."*

This method is effective because people are less prone to get defensive when you talk about yourself. The moment you make the issue about them, they will respond negatively or become disillusioned. The listener/listeners will be more open, responsive and accepting to the idea of reflecting upon what you are trying to communicate, even when it isn't positive.

Similarly, you reduce the chances of arguing with the other person about who is right. Since you mention things related to yourself, they aren't debatable, which minimizes the scope for conflict. On the contrary, if you say things about the listener, they are likelier to get defensive or argumentative by challenging your view. When we talk about ourselves, we shut doors for the other person to dispute it.

Refrain from being a yes-man

Being an effective communicator is not about agreeing to everything everyone says. Rather, it is about how you disagree with them without offending them. This is especially true for people who are not confident or possess a high sense of self-esteem. You may be socially awkward or easily intimated by others. Even when you don't wish you, you will go with whatever others say without expressing your needs or preferences. If you identify with this, it is time you learn to talk for yourself or take a courteous yet firm or assertive stand about your needs and preferences.

Assertiveness and aggressiveness are not the same though you may think there is a thin line between them. Assertiveness is a person's ability to stand up for themselves while staying polite, respectful, courteous and non-offensive. It is about arriving at a win-win, where neither other people nor your needs are overlooked. Aggression is more about 'I win, you lose,' while assertiveness is about, 'everyone wins.' You are not obligated to be a people pleaser, and that should reflect in your communication patterns.

Speak to people in a logical and balanced manner without attacking them if you think your needs are not being met or you want to state your preferences. For example, if you say something such as, *"I prefer going street market hopping than visiting high-end boutiques for shopping"*. You are stating your needs and preferences rather than giving orders about, which sounds more acceptable and balanced to the listener. It is about expressing your views, needs, ideas, and preferences in a genuine and healthy manner to arrive at some win-win situation.

When you are stating your preferences, you are still leaving scope for the other person to express their opinion and preferences. When you establish both your and another person's needs, the opportunity of arriving at a win-win situation is higher. Say a courteous yet firm *"no"* when you are not up for doing something. Politely turn down any requests by saying no when you don't want to do something.

Assertiveness is integral to the process of being an ace communicator. It involves standing up for your values and beliefs while being unafraid of articulating your desires, needs, and goals to others. Assertiveness in communication involves putting everyone on an equal footing and focusing on mutual respect. There is no intention on your part to hurt or offend others, just like you will not accept other people hurting, offending or undermining you. The focus is on mutual respect and arriving at a win-win situation for everyone involved.

Here are some valuable tips for boosting your assertiveness quotient. See others as force you to need to collaborate or work with instead of work against. When you are facing any challenging situation in any aspect of your life with certain people, focus on collaboration or solution rather than competition and one-upmanship. Even if you end up winning the argument, you may lose the relationship. Effective communication is utilizing every challenging situation to strengthen your connection with a person. This helps us leave a positive impression on people once the challenging situation is behind us.

Think about this carefully. Each time we launch into an argument or a fight with our partner/spouse, we view it as a *"me versus him or her"* war. Look at the challenge from a point that you are both in one team, and the enemy is the challenge you are facing as a couple. Effective communication is about working towards a common solution instead of trying to figure out who is right. This one technique alone will help you enjoy more effective communication in your interpersonal relationships. Stay assertive, while focusing on the bigger picture or greater good. Instead of perceiving everyone who does not agree with you as an enemy, see them as an ally you can work with to arrive at a win-win solution.

Consciously develop the habit of stating your needs, feelings, opinions, and preferences openly. You don't always have to go with whatever people say. If you have a slightly varied preference or perspective, clarify it. One of the biggest blunders we make when it comes to communication in intimate and interpersonal relationships is that we always assume that the other person should automatically know our needs or understand our feelings without us having to articulate it. Stay honest, transparent, respectful and courteous when it comes to expressing your needs. While ordering a sandwich at the café, would you rather for a ham cheese sandwich or ham on rye with tomatoes, extra cheddar, cucumber and less of lettuce? Obviously, the second one! Then, why are we afraid to express our needs, opinions, and preferences in our personal, professional and social relationships?

Do not feel guilty about standing up for your own needs or preferences. When something isn't compatible with your beliefs, values, preferences, and priorities, refuse without regretting it. Kill the guilt. Replace this guilt with constructive or positive self-talk. If you refuse a friend who is constantly borrowing money from you without taking responsibility for their life, there isn't a need to think, *"I am a terrible person because I am not helping my friend"*. Rather think along the lines of, *"I deserve to take care of my interests and monetary stability without comprising on my overall financial security"*.

Another clever tip for eliminating the guilt while being assertive and saying no to people is to imagine yourself standing up for someone you care about deeply. Would you let anyone do something similar with your loved one? No? We are likelier to take a stand when it is about a loved one. It gets much easier to talk for someone we care about deeply instead of ourselves.

Always use beginning with *"I"* rather than *"you"*, where you take onus for your feelings instead of accusing another person.

Failure to recognize and adapt to someone's communication style

Identifying a person's communication style is integral to the process of effective communication, while also reducing instances of conflicts and misunderstanding. Here are fundamental communication styles that you can adapt to or manage for accomplishing more fulfilling, balanced and harmonious relationships.

Assertive communicators – Assertive communicators are folks who are high on self-confidence and self-esteem. Assertiveness is known to be the most balanced and healthiest communication style, which seeks to find a middle path between being too aggressive or passive, while also keeping away from manipulation tactics.

Assertive people know their limits, and do not take too well to being pushed around by people who wish to get them to do certain things that they don't want to. At the same time, they will rarely violate other's feelings to meet their objectives. This is a win-win communication style since assertive communicators almost always think of solutions that are advantageous to everyone involved instead of only thinking about themselves.

Typical characteristics of an assertive communicator are the ability to achieve their goals without hurting other people. They strive to preserve their own rights while also being mindful and respectful of other's rights. They have high social and emotional expressiveness. Assertive communicators like to make their own choices, while also accepting responsibility for these choices.

Typical non-verbal behavior of assertive communicators is a medium voice pitch, volume and speech rate. Notice that their posture will almost always be open and relaxed. They will stand tall and barely demonstrate signs of nervousness. Their gestures are more expansive, open and receptive.

Assertive people like to maintain eye contact and a more spatial position, which communicates that they are control of their actions and respectful towards other people. Typical things said by them include something, *"Please will you lower the speed? I am trying to drink some water"* or *"I apologize I can't assist you with your homework since I have an appointment with my dentist scheduled for this evening"*. Try to adopt an assertive style of communication if you want to be effective.

Aggressive communicators – You wish you didn't have to deal with these types of communicators, but unfortunately, they exist everywhere. This communication style is all about winning, mostly at the cost of other people. When someone is overly aggressive in their communication, you can use assertiveness to stand up for yourself.

Aggressive communicators will always hold their needs, preferences, beliefs, opinions, views, and desires over others. They act like they possess greater rights than other people and are entitled to decide for everyone around them. Aggressive communicators are often so fixated on their delivery of what they are trying to say that the message is eventually lost.

The typical non-verbal behavior pattern of aggressive communicators includes speaking in an unusually high volume, keeping a wider and more expansive posture than others around them to signify power and occupy more physical space. Their facial expressions are often rapid and jerk. The language they use is along the lines of *"Don't you understand such a simple or basic thing?"* or *"This has to be done exactly as I say or my way"* or *"you drive me mad"*. Aggressive communicators are adept in the art of blaming, calling people names, criticizing, insulting, taunting, threatening and being sarcastic to feel good about themselves.

Passive aggressive communicators look passive on the surface for it but play out their frustration or rage behind the scenes. They are almost always grappling with feelings of powerlessness and resentment. Passive aggressive communicators will generally say things like, *"why don't you take over the project. My inputs are anyway not valued"* or *"you know more than others anyway, you should be the one heading the project"*. There is a dash of sarcasm in everything they say, which stems from a feeling of resentment and frustration.

What is the body language of a passive-aggressive person? They will talk in a sugary sweet tone while marinating an asymmetrical posture and quick facial expressions as well as gestures that on the surface look innocent. Their spatial position comprises standing close enough to make the other person feel uncomfortable. Sometimes, they will lightly touch others, while pretending to be warm, welcoming and friendly.

Submissive communicators – Submissive communicators are people pleasers. They will do just about anything to avoid a confrontation or displeasing people at any expense. They tend to bend backward in their bid to place other people's needs, wants, desires, opinions, beliefs, and preferences before theirs. Submissive communicators often operate under the belief that their needs are not as important as those of others around them. This leads to plenty of frustration and disappointment. The language used by a submissive communicator includes something along the lines of, *"Oh! It's fine. I don't really want it now"* or *"you can choose whatever you want, anything is fine with me"*.

The body language of submissive communicators includes speaking using a soft tone, employing a diminutive head-down position, fidgeting or nervous gestures and a posture that makes them look much lower in stature than other people. Their body language is marked by a victim mentality.

Manipulative communicator – These are probably the shrewdest, most scheming and dangerous of all communicators. They are calculating and often prey on other's emotions for serving their own purpose. Manipulative communicators have the ability to influence, coerce and control others for their own benefit. The words and phrases they say always have some underlying meaning or hidden motive, which their unfortunate victims are not aware of.

The typical things they say include, *"You are indeed fortunate enough to enjoy their lovely pastries. I wish I was as fortunate as you to have them too. I can't really afford these expensive pastries"* or *"I didn't get the time to buy anything, so I didn't have any option but to put on this dress. I am just hoping that I don't look too bad in it. I wish I had something else to wear"*. Their voice is generally patronizing, often going in the direction of high-pitched, while the facial expressions are more 'hang dog' types.

Closed minds

How many times have we faced the frustrating prospect of interacting with people who filter everything we say through the lens of their own biases, preconceived notions, myopic beliefs, and prejudices? Doesn't it act as a hindrance to the process of effective communication? Everyone operates with its own set of values, viewpoints, and beliefs. However, staying inflexible and rigid about your views does stops us from hearing or learning something new about the speaker or being open to what they are trying to communicate. Avoid operating with pre-held views and beliefs that prevent you from gaining new insights about an individual or situation.

Not everyone you talk to is going to hold similar views and beliefs as you. Empathy, understanding, and considerateness are the biggest factors of positive communication. When we see things from the other person's point of view, we understand where they come from even if we do not necessarily agree with them. The objective of mastering interpersonal skills and active listening is to keep our minds open, flexible and accepting. Try to put yourself in the other person's shoes to develop more understanding of their situation or views. People who disagree with you need not be wrong. Not all people share your situation or circumstances. Try to think from the other person's perspective to understand their situation or views more effectively.

Today's world is a melting pot of cultures, ethnicities, abilities, religions, sexual orientations, political views and much more' Classifying and labeling people using sweeping generalizations can kill the process of effective communication. It is easier and takes much less effort to place people in different mental boxes that we've prepared.

However, in the long run, it doesn't help build meaningful relationships. One of the biggest signs of an effective communicator is the ability to understand, consider and appreciate varied views even when they do not necessarily match with our own. Make a sincere effort to know people rather than judging them. Avoid assuming things unless you have clear evidence. Assumptions are the biggest stumbling blocks of communication and listening. We render the process of communication ineffective by resorting to generalizations and assumptions. It hampers the opportunity of knowing and understanding people.

Make a sincere effort to understand the other person's unique background, overall life experiences and personality traits while listening. Develop a practice of meeting and interacting with new people from different places or cultures. Give others the space and comfort for freely expressing their views. Take time to consider other people's views. Take into consideration the other's expectations, views, and needs while communicating. Stay assertive without getting disrespectful.

When you don't agree with someone as we discussed earlier saying something such as *"Now, this is a really different or unique way of looking at things, which I hadn't considered earlier. I am intrigued. Can you please tell me why you think like this?"* You don't necessarily agree with the other person, but you are still open the door for sharing or exchanging views and increasing your own understanding about why people think the way they do. Communication and social intelligence are about adapting to different personalities, cultures, views, societies and more to form healthy and meaningful personal, professional and social relationships. Every time you are tempted to argue or disagree with other people.

The stuck records

Some folks are inclined to go on and on like a stuck record that the other person switches off mentally or stops responding (remember the traffic signal technique in an earlier chapter). There is only so much we can focus on for a given time span without being bored or distracted. Long-winded, verbose and wordy sentences that never seem to end can tire the listener, focusing him/her on switching off. Avoid rambling. Use a full mental stop once you are done conveying your message. Give the other person an opportunity to process the information and clarify their understanding. To gauge the listener's initial understanding, make a statement, followed by a question. One of the biggest communication blunders people make is speaking without offering the listener an opportunity to give their take, process the information or clarify their understanding of what they (the speaker) said.

Observe how people become ineffective communicators by communicating the same point using different words. They will restructure what they are trying to communicate until it becomes redundant. If you believe the other person has not comprehended what you are communicating, use meta-communication. This implies you are offering your comments on a conversation to get a person to open up.

For instance, if you get the idea that the other person isn't reacting to a vital message say something to the effect of, *"Hey, I observe that you are not responding/reacting to what I just said. However, I feel it is vital and relevant to our overall team performance.*

How come?" This offers us an opportunity to understand why the listener has switched off. You will know if the person was able to understand what you said.

Rather than trying to say one thing using different words because you get the idea that the other person has not comprehended what you are trying to communicate, utilize meta-communication to do a quick check-in of their understanding.

Conclusion

Thank you for choosing this book.

I genuinely hope it has offered you several techniques, pointers, and strategies for communicating effectively across many settings to enjoy more lasting, meaningful, gratifying and fulfilling relationships.

The objective of the book is to help you get rid of your fears, nervousness and lack of confidence to take on the world in a more self-assured and effective manner, one communication skill at a time. Communication is the master key to building solid, rewarding and lasting relationships along with impacting your chances of success in life.
The book also helps you understand the finer details required for communicating effectively with people, including building listening skills.

The next step is to start using strategies mentioned in the book right away. Information has to be translated into knowledge, which in turn is translated into experience and wisdom. Of course, you won't transform from an awkward, shy or inhibited communicator into a communication pro overnight. However, one step a time you'll get closer to your goal if you work on it in a disciplined and consistent. With implementation and practice, you can steadily but definitely transform into a communication force to reckon with.

Finally, if you enjoyed reading the book, please take the time to share your views by posting a review of Amazon. It'd be highly appreciated!

CPSIA information can be obtained
at www.ICGtesting.com
Printed in the USA
LVHW091529050919
630055LV00029B/718/P

9 781080 939602